UNIVERSAL
SKEPTICISM

UNIVERSAL
SKEPTICISM

TAKING THE LYING OUT OF LIVING, BOOK TWO

KEVIN HENLEY

To order additional copies of this book, contact:
Xlibris Corporation
1-888-795-4274
www.Xlibris.com
Orders@Xlibris.com
21289

CONTENTS

THIS BOOK IS DEDICATED TO ALL THOSE PEOPLE
FOR WHOM FREEDOM IS SYNONYMOUS WITH
THE ABSENCE OF PAROCHIALISM.

INTRODUCTION

"Taking the Lying out of Living: The Skeptic's Manifesto" was such an interesting book to write that I have decided to add a sequel. My original text was published back in 2001 as a kind of antidote to all of the misleading systems of ideas that professional liars are constantly using to deceive everyone around them.

In my first book "for unrepentant skeptics", I touched on many different aspects of human life, including psychology, politics, business, education, justice and science. As I wrote on the jacket, I drew on "both history and current events to concisely demonstrate just how inadequate all the world's most important religions and ideologies are when it comes to solving the problems that beset us . . . A healthy dose of skepticism makes every problem that much easier to handle, by taking the lying out of living." Although that book was an excellent introduction to the principles of universal skepticism, I feel that it left a number of important things unsaid.

This, then, is Book Two, covering ground that was left unexplored the first time around. Without repeating any of my earlier observations, I want to strengthen and to deepen my investigation of the human condition, by trying to find out why most human beings, even in the richer countries, do not succeed in living very satisfactory lives.

There are in fact many millions of fed-up people out there, not just in North America but all over the world. Ranting and raving about everything which has gone wrong in society has become very popular recently, with some people getting upset about all the disgusting things that those currently in power are doing, while others keep trying to stick the blame on the opposition instead. Neither attitude is particularly edifying.

So far as I can tell, universal skepticism is the only way in which we who have so often been deceived in the past can free ourselves from the tyranny of believing in any of the ideas our oppressors have been using in order to bolster their domination. This emphatically includes not only those tyrants who are currently running the world, but also all those who say that they want to run it differently, because when the opposition gets into power they always end up breaking their promises and doing more or less the same things that their predecessors did.

Another way of phrasing the approximately same idea is to point out that today's liberators are tomorrow's persecutors, something which has already happened thousands of times in history. For example, the communists were supposed to save everyone from capitalist tyranny and ended up turning dozens of countries into gulags. The democrats, on the other hand, were supposed to save the world from communist tyranny and brought back robber barons instead. Whenever the opposition to something or other gets into power, it always and forever creates a new version of whatever it was supposed to have been opposing. In such a world, it is no wonder that millions of people are getting more and more upset about everything all of the time.

In fact, what is surprising about all the ranting and raving going on nowadays is not that it is finally happening, but that it was not as pronounced in the past. After all, what gets everyone so upset is not new at all; it is just most people's social impotence. Most of us have almost no control whatsoever over our lives, partly because human beings have always been locked into a rigid geological, biological, sociological and psychological environment whose ultimate confines many of us are only just beginning to notice.

To take an extreme example, if I decide that I do not like it so much here on Earth this year and that I would really like to spend a few months roaming around Andromeda galaxy, too bad for me. There is no way that I could ever get there or even anywhere remotely near it. As a matter of fact, I could never hope to go farther than an ordinary Earth-bound jet goes when it is on its way from one airport to another. The truth is that no human beings have ever gone farther than the Moon, while only a select few are allowed to board global orbiters.

Believe it or not, most of the people on this planet have not yet even boarded an airplane. The same type of comparison also applies to other technological freedoms, such as using the Internet or even the ordinary telephone. Most human beings are also powerless in all sorts of non-technical ways, having been denied the capacity to control their own lives in any significant way. The various different sorts of discrimination (gender, race, class) keep 99% of the world's population away from more than a minimal use of even any of the existing, rather-limited technologies.

The fact is that those few opportunities to act that do exist have almost all been gobbled up by the several hundred thousand people on this planet who make all the important decisions. Even in the nominally free-enterprise democracies, less than one-tenth of one percent of the total population has any discernible access to real decision-making. As a result, almost everyone else is fully justified in being absolutely furious all the time.

This is abundantly true for all of the world's poor people, which is to say the majority of those who live in Asia, Africa, Latin America and Eastern Europe, as well as significant minorities of people living in North America, Western Europe and Australasia. What is surprising about the almost six billion poor people in the world is that they are not always upset. Given the disgusting conditions that they have to live under all the time, it is amazing that there are so proportionately few rebellions, or that there do not seem to be that many suicide epidemics taking place. Russia is about the only poor country around in which millions of people no longer seem to want to stay alive.

Furious impotence, therefore, is the only emotion which is really appropriate for the enormous numbers of really poor people who are missing out on society's limited technical capacity to take good care of everybody. But furious impotence is also a reality for middle-class people wherever they exist. Even though they are far better off than most of the world's population, none of them are even remotely connected to those very few people who have any power; if they were connected, they would not be in the middle class any more. The fact is that none of them, neither the poor nor the middle-class people, make any of the decisions which most affect all of our everyday lives.

For example, the vast majority of people have no input whatsoever into whether or not the USA or any of its allies go to war, be that in Panama, in Somalia, in Serbia, in Afghanistan, in Iraq, in North Korea, or in any other non-conformist state. The poor or the middle-class can decide to support such a war, or to oppose such a war, but the people who make the real decisions do so for their own reasons, which normally have nothing to do with what ordinary people may or may not think about that. 99% of the time, the minds of powerless people can be sufficiently well-manipulated anyway so that their collective points of view can be safely ignored by those in power. The effect of such wars on the economy or on the prices of ordinary commodities can change the daily lives of ordinary poor or middle-class people drastically, but that does not mean that they have any real impact on the decision-making itself.

The same thing is true about investment, which is in no way controlled by any middle-class people, let alone poor ones. Stock-market trends do not benefit powerless people in any significant ways. Like the poor people who are always buying lottery tickets, one or two individuals may end up being lucky, but the system is set up mainly to benefit house investors, which means the major investors who control most of the operations. Even middle-class people's pension funds are in the hands of professional managers, who make decisions based either on hare-brained schemes of grandeur or on the relative size of their own stock options. No one in the middle-class, let alone the poor class, even knows for sure whether or not he or she will even have a pension, come retirement time.

And so on down the line. Nothing of any importance that happens in politics, international, national or local, nothing which happens with regard to any aspect of the economy, nothing which concerns any significant social or cultural matters, nothing at all over which human beings have any control is decided by anyone outside the realms of power. If millions of people are in a permanent state of rage, that rage is therefore entirely legitimate and normal. Consequently, if anyone who does not belong to the ruling class is not completely upset, he or she must be either totally brainwashed or thoroughly masochistic.

As for brainwashing, all of our illustrious rulers always try to channel legitimate rage away from themselves, in all sorts of illegitimate directions. Going to war every now and then is one of their favorite methods of distraction. But taking out our misplaced anger at tin-pot dictators left over from the Cold War, like Slobodan Milosevic, Saddam Hussein and Kim Il-Jung, is completely worthless because none of those axes of evil ever have nearly as much power as do any of the real rulers.

The people who really rule the world are those who manage other people by managing their money, mainly through business transactions but also through government spending. In the richest countries, such as the USA, only a relatively small proportion of the Gross National Product is related to government expenditure, even if all levels of government are taken into account. Most of the problem therefore relates to business transactions, the vast majority of which are speculative, having nothing to do with the physical economy.

Other countries have larger or smaller percentages of government expenditure, but political corruption, which is widespread everywhere, ensures that private enterprise controls just about everything that moves. Being upset all the time at these money managers, the real troublemakers, is the only sane posture known, while blaming any lesser lights or worse yet, blaming completely powerless people, is crazy. Not getting upset at all, by letting some rich people control everything that happens in our lives, is even more psychotic.

This is why it is so incredibly ridiculous when some world leader says that "we" have to overthrow some particular dictator in order to impose freedom and democracy on some foreign country. This is not only absurd because it is patently impossible to force another culture to become democratic, nor only because invasions always take place for economic and geopolitical reasons which have nothing to do with freedom and democracy. Even the fact that, according to polls published during the weeks leading up to some of these wars, the majority of the people in the invading countries were also initially opposed to military action, is irrelevant.

Much more to the point is the fact that world leaders never in fact consult any powerless people, in the USA or anywhere else, before they make their grandiose decisions. The majority of the population is never really consulted in advance, but is only allowed to support the initiative once it has been undertaken, even if that means having to change their minds almost completely. This is because democracies are not really very democratic and the people in them are not free in any real sense.

The places that are normally called democracies in this world are indeed more democratic than official dictatorships, whether these are national-socialist dictatorships like Saddam Hussein's used to be or communist dictatorships like China's still is. Most of the people living in democratic countries like the USA and France are also freer than most of those living in dictatorships, or in theocracies like Iran. But simplistic comparisons like these do not eliminate the much more important fact that all countries on this planet are light-years away from anything remotely resembling genuine freedom and democracy.

At first glance, the differences between democracies and dictatorships seem very large, since freedom of expression appears to be entirely present in some countries and entirely absent in others. Like the distance between Europe and the Americas a century ago, or the distance between the Earth and the Moon more recently, the freedoms to be found in democratic countries seem very different from the direct tyranny of dictatorships. Looked at on a larger or more fundamental scale, however, those differences seem less imposing, just like the distance between the Earth and the Moon diminishes to almost nothing when compared to the distance between the Earth and the Sun, or to the much greater distance between the solar system and the next nearest galaxy.

Money and power divide those who really do have freedom from those who do not, which means that the so-called democratic countries are really plutocracies, in which people with a lot of money and a lot of power have all the freedom that human beings can muster, while those with less money and power have less freedom, and those with no money and no power have no freedom at all. Genuine democracy cannot in fact exist in countries run by money and power, in which government and business leaders in no way resemble the majority of the population.

In fact, people in democracies have their freedoms until they need them (Bertrand Russell), since those freedoms are always taken away in times of crisis. But powerless people are not at all free even at the best of times. For one thing, the neo-conservative morons who currently run the world actually seem to believe that any government which really tries to act in the best interests of the majority of its people must be a communist government! The neo-conservative equation between power and money has become so popular in most officially democratic countries that millions of ordinary people seem proud to be ignored or mistreated by their rulers. Events such as the 2003 invasion of Iraq are therefore a kind of cruel joke, since they inevitably make life more difficult for ordinary people, whether or not they supported the initial decision.

Unfortunately, a lot of powerless but misguided people are victims of false consciousness and seem to enjoy being bossed around. They like being told that they cannot cross certain borders, ostensibly "for their own security", or that they have to submit to all sorts of airport controls which apply to airline passengers but not to rich people on private planes, nor even to airline pilots, baggage handlers or security guards. For some strange reason, they feel better knowing that there are huge areas of their own countries which are off-limits to ordinary people like themselves. They are foolishly reassured when governments, armies, bureaucrats and private corporations refuse to allow them access to tons of restricted information, especially when it is useful information about the lives of ordinary people!

Sometimes, they even seem to revel in the understanding that dozens of obscure lobbies, secret societies and old boys' networks in fact control everything that moves. They give the impression that they enjoy letting the rich and the famous run the world, as well as submitting to every form of discrimination known to mankind. And they support that theory by saying that letting ordinary people run their own lives is impossible and unrealistic.

To be sure, this is true enough in many instances. Some ordinary (powerless) people misuse the little bit of freedom and democracy that they sometimes possess by foolishly imitating the rich and the powerful. They buy huge trucks with four-wheel drives just to go back and forth to work all by themselves. They speculate on the market in their own stupid way by scooping up millions of lottery tickets, thereby paying a voluntary tax. They get very upset at school taxes and highway tolls while still supporting much more expensive military budgets.

Still, decisions made by people in power are potentially much more damaging than those made by powerless people. However, even though mistakes made by the rich and the powerful cost thousands of times more to society than those made by ordinary people, it is still true that nothing that critics and skeptics have to say about that will probably change anything. The most that skeptics can ask for is that those who let the big-shots run everything should at least be honest about it.

Stop using words like freedom and democracy except in a relative way. Point out that this particular country in which we find ourselves may be freer and more democratic than a whole lot of other places, but that it may also be less free than some other countries out there. Freely admit that no human society anywhere has ever been able to control the rich and the powerful all that much. Finally, try to explain, as I am doing, why it is that even though everyone is supposedly born equal, a few individuals turn out being more equal than all the others (George Orwell).

TOXIC LEADERSHIP

In my first book, I blamed the world's egomaniacs for most of this social impotence. I called the maniacal rulers of society "disordered personalities", and defined them as those dominators who use belief systems (religions and ideologies) in order to get others to do their bidding. I was in fact trying to give both a psychological and a sociological definition of evil, which largely depends on the sadistic domination of social institutions by those in power.

Since that book was published, I found out that the people I called disordered personalities are exactly the same people who French psychiatrist Marie-France Hirigoyen has referred to as "toxic personalities". In her international best-seller, "Stalking the Soul: Emotional Abuse and the Erosion of Identity", Hirigoyen described how the toxic personalities among us offset the fundamental lovelessness of their own lives by victimizing others, turning talented and sensitive people into nervous wrecks through constant harassment. Although Hirigoyen wrote her book mainly in order to help her patients defend themselves against dominating spouses and dominating managers, she also had the perspicacity to conclude that in a system based on the survival of the fittest, perverse egomaniacs in fact run the entire world and all of its institutions.

Unfortunately, so far as I can tell, all social systems are based on some form of "survival of the fittest". Even though that particular expression originally sprang from the robber-baron social-Darwinism of the late nineteenth century, I think that toxic personalities have always dominated human society from the very beginning and that they are every bit as powerful in socialist or theocratic societies as they are in capitalist ones. The perverse egomaniacs who run the world always see themselves as being the fittest, "the best and the brightest", no matter in what kind of social system they may be operating. They really seem to think that successfully ruining other people's lives is what makes them supremely qualified to rule us.

Apparently, in Zimbabwe, they refer to this situation as a "kakistocracy", which means government by the worst people. But the problem is not just about government as such. So far as I can tell, all human institutions are kakistocracies, all the governments but also all the businesses and all the unions and all the associations, every social structure ever founded. It seems that every time human beings get together in groups, every form of society always ends up being run by the worst people in it. Once again, as the baseball coach (Leo Durocher) put it, "nice guys finish last".

The origins of this human disaster probably go way back in time, to Neolithic, Mesolithic or even to Paleolithic society, long before the first urban civilizations began. It most likely has something to do with the emergence of a division of labor, between the chiefs and the ordinary natives, when dominant personalities first began bossing others around. But it does not really matter which came first, the chicken or the egg; in this case the first division of labor or the first toxic individuals, the result has been just as devastating.

Ever since that time, toxic personalities have been constantly ripping off other people's ideas, taking credit for other people's work, appropriating other people's wealth for themselves, or starting wars that they themselves do not have to fight. Once they succeed in reducing their victims to social impotence by using constant physical or psychological bludgeoning, they then have the temerity to proclaim their own social excellence and to give each other peace prizes and Nobel prizes and every other sort of medal and recognition.

Other people allow this to happen because they identify with the delinquent rulers as successful aggressors. Even those who would never personally mistreat others to the extent that the toxic personalities do, nevertheless support their harmful behavior out of fear, or even more often out of emulation for those who dare to be difficult. Most people have some sort of mystique about leaders which sees them as being highly qualified and necessarily egotistical. Ordinary, powerless people often get vicarious pleasure out of watching a disordered personality ruin someone else's life, something that they would never dare to do on their own. In this way, they imitate most judges in politically correct countries, who are constantly letting guilty people off the hook so that they can ruin even more innocent lives.

Many victims also let toxic personalities get away with whatever evil they may be perpetrating because of hope. Rather than confront a difficult situation head on, masochistic victims put up with their misery in the hope that the sadists will eventually go away and leave them alone. Unfortunately, this is something which almost never happens in the real world, making hope into a useless or even a harmful emotion, one of the most important roots of all evil.

This is what makes the Stockholm syndrome humanity's most important problem. Apparently, the current name for this syndrome came from a bank robbery which took place in the capital of Sweden a few decades ago, during which the hostages tried to bargain for their freedom by making friends and even having sex with their captors! But the identification of victims with perpetrators, in the name of social harmony, has been going on forever. It is exactly the same problem that was addressed in the film, "Night Porter", in which a Jewish woman made out with her Nazi tormentor, an obvious metaphor for all of the Jewish Kapos in the concentration camps who helped the Nazis control the other Jews, or for the rich Jews in Hungary who sold the poor Jews to the Germans in exchange for their own lives (Ben Hecht).

It is also the same disease which was described by the North African psychiatrist, Albert Memmi, as the colonial syndrome, in which millions of colonial peoples all over the world imitated their European, American and Japanese overlords even to the extent of writing poems and painting pictures depicting objects from the "mother" country, which did not even exist in the colonial world. This is the evil disease of false reconciliation, based on the disgusting premise that might makes right, and is certainly the number one method used by all the dominators who run the world.

Moreover, these toxic personalities seem to be the same people who

Pierre-Joseph Proudhon was talking about when he observed that property is theft. I would like to enlarge Proudhon's idea somewhat by pointing out that it applies to much more than just economic exploitation. In economics, this nineteenth-century idea simply meant that since the economy is a cooperative undertaking, individual profit-making has to take place as an uninvited subtraction from the collective enterprise: in other words, theft. A milder way of saying about the same thing would be to look at profit as a bribe granted by society to entrepreneurs for their exploitation of some economic opportunity, resulting indirectly in the creation of a common good or service. Inevitably, the successful investor or merchant ends up "making" more money than what the rest of society gets back in return.

Prior to the rise of free-enterprise capitalism, the aristocracy ran the world, using their ownership of large agricultural estates and their control of all the world's kingdoms and empires in order to lord it over all the other social classes. Since commercial capitalism first came into play, however, there has been a long-term tendency for governments to be gradually shunted aside so that individual investors could take more direct control of everything.

The unfortunate part of all economic reality throughout recorded history is that no one has so far been able to figure out a way to provide goods and services without everyone having to put up with the bribe or the theft of common property, either by government or by private enterprise. This helps to explain why private investors know that all current governments are corrupt and inefficient, since they are the ones whose constant commercial lobbying has made those governments so corrupt and inefficient!

As I pointed out in my first book, all of the historical attempts at building a better world have simply resulted in new versions of the old disease: the aristocracy being replaced with private capitalism, private capitalism often being replaced with state capitalism (fascist, communist or social-democratic governments), and then back again to private capitalism. Directly or indirectly, we are stuck with either the power motive or the profit motive as the only methods of leadership available and it makes no moral difference whatever if the profiteers or power-mongers are private individuals or government bureaucrats, aristocrats or capitalists.

However, enlarging Proudhon's idea about theft means applying it to every social situation and not just to economic realities. It is not just property which is stolen, but prestige and recognition and ideas as well. The toxic personalities of this world are not just misappropriating everyone else's goods; they are also misappropriating everyone else's entire lives. As Hirigoyen pointed out, the dominating egomaniac in a family or on the job steals the victim's sense of self-worth and the victim's place in society just as much as he or she steals the victim's worldly possessions. Domination is especially disastrous at the apex of society, but it also exists at subordinate levels, in the various kinds of pecking orders described by modern sociology.

Not surprisingly, this is also the theme of much of the world's most important literature and cinema. One of the most interesting examples of this comes from Quebec, where one of the most popular fictional characters is called Seraphin, an archetypical miser who lords it over everyone in his local neighborhood. This character was originally created during the 1930s by Claude-Henri Grignon and the setting of his novel ("A Man and His Sins") was a typical pioneer village in the Laurentian Mountains. In this imagined village, local farmers were forced to eke out a miserable pittance while being simultaneously exploited by the Catholic Church and the local politicians. Seraphin was the most important local big-shot whose close ties with those in power made it easy for him to make a fortune by ruining everyone else's lives, most notably by purchasing a beautiful young girl from her destitute father, forcing her to become his long-suffering wife.

In the recent movie version of this story, Seraphin was eventually ruined when one of his victims managed to get away with burning his house down, along with everything in it. But this is only a Quebecois version of a story which crops up in almost every culture, often with the same kind of Walt Disney-like happy ending which concludes the Seraphin tale. Charles Dickens' nineteenth-century story, "Oliver Twist", is another good example, in which the bad guys (Fagin and Bill) eventually get their improbable come-uppance. Another well-known example is the 1939 American film, "Mr. Smith goes to Washington", in which a young senator is constantly being manipulated by all of the occult forces in American politics. Once again, the writers had to introduce a phony happy ending in order to get the movie shown all across the USA and around the world.

In real life, however, the usual ending is that the bad guys of this world succeed right through to the end with all of their nefarious schemes and start numerous political, economic and social dynasties by passing on the proceeds of their evil natures to their offspring. Even cultural legacies can be passed on in this way, as the careers of most of the world's religious leaders can attest. Centuries after the deaths of such founders as Moses, Confucius, Guatama, Jesus or Mohamed, today's big-shots are still profiting from those religions in order to help them exploit their own victims nowadays.

But as in the free-enterprise economy denounced by Proudhon, the most important observation arising from discussions about all human societies is simply the futility of it all. No solution to this fundamental problem seems to exist. So far as I can tell, there is no way out of the cycle of exploitation which does not simultaneously create a new version of the old problem. Human beings simply have to put up with all sorts of unfortunate realities, such as this one, as part of the human condition.

Unfortunately, professional Pollyannas of every sort always dismiss honest observations of this nature precisely because they do not provide any happy ending which can make everyone feel good. Books and articles written by hundreds of critical intellectuals in every country in the world are always being rejected by apologists for the powerful. Sycophantic reviewers are constantly dismissing these authors because while they are strong on criticism of society, they are weak on solutions. But Pollyanna rejection of reality turns out to be the easiest cop-out of all. When no solutions appear to exist, it is simply wishful thinking or belief in magic to pretend otherwise.

This same type of goody-goody thinking takes place whenever "truth and reconciliation" commissions are appointed after some kind of major crime against humanity has been committed. For example, after apartheid was dismantled in South Africa, the new government set up the most well-known of such commissions. The idea was to give amnesty to every one of the guilty parties in exchange for their revealing all of the crimes that they had committed in the past. Once all the crimes were out in the open, this was supposed to cleanse the country of past misdeeds and to enable everyone to get on with their lives. The same kind of amnesty has also been declared recently in dozens of other similar situations, all over the world. Perpetrators and victims are supposed to live peacefully, side by side, for ever after, just because everyone now knows exactly who did what to whom.

Nevertheless, this kind of artificial happy ending has no basis in reality. All that happens is that the bad guys on both sides of every conflict have successfully gotten away with their evil deeds while the victims have to "grin and bear it" forever. Even Canadian writer Erna Paris, in her extremely revealing book called "Long Shadows: Truth, Lies and History", was eventually tempted by the happy-ending scenario. Paris wrote almost 500 pages of well-researched text to show how different countries nowadays have treated recent periods in their history in which major crimes against humanity were committed: Germany and France during the Holocaust, Japan during the same period, South Africa during apartheid, the USA during racial segregation, Serbia during the wars against secession, and so on.

In each case, Paris showed how the guilty parties were never really punished for their misdeeds and how each country has more or less successfully whitewashed its history so as not to emphasize the rotten parts. But even Paris concludes that mastering the past leads to some kind of imperfect justice. In the real world, however, no homilies of any sort, no turning of the other cheek, can ever erase the fact that the toxic personalities have succeeded in imposing their will on their victims.

But it is not just in extreme situations like war that no happy endings are ever encountered; the same observation also applies to everyday life. Those who like to call themselves the fittest survive basically by becoming society's leaders, which means those whose goal it is to appropriate everyone else's contributions to society. By spending their entire lives organizing and manipulating everyone else, rather than doing any real work, these people end up controlling everything which exists and trying to make everyone else's lives as miserable and as loveless as their own.

The rest of us have to choose between joining the bad guys and becoming part of the problem, like the middle-class hypocrite did in the

1992 American film "Falling Down", or by becoming one of the victims and therefore finishing last. In every area of life, a person is either a victim or a perpetrator, and no amount of rhetorical posturing is ever going to change that fact.

To give a banal example, if a person's car runs into a pothole in the street, it could turn out to be nobody's fault, especially if that pothole is the only one on that street and has only been there for a short time. In many neighborhoods, however, there are dozens of potholes in every street and most of them are allowed to ruin people's cars for weeks or months on end. Many streets were poorly constructed in the first place, while others have been allowed to deteriorate for ages. Most of the time, the pothole problem has been caused, or compounded, by some negligent individual, who most often turns out to be someone who is profiting from other people's broken axles.

Unfortunately, the pothole story is only one example among thousands of others. The same sort of thing takes place not only when private fortunes and political dynasties are involved, but even with grand ideas whose original goal seems to have been to free people from all of this murkiness. For example, an objective reading of the New Testament would lead any honest person to conclude that its Christian authors intended to found a genuinely communist society, in which the meek would inherit the Earth because it is easier for a camel to go through the eye of a needle than for a rich man to enter the kingdom of God. Shortly after the New Testament was written, however, Christianity stopped being a religion for poor people and instead became the governing religion of the Roman Empire. It has been used by popes, emperors and presidents ever since in order to help sadistic leaders control hundreds of millions of new victims.

This is particularly ironic in the case of fundamentalist Christianity, especially prevalent in the USA, which has somehow managed to use the gospel in order to promote the free-enterprise ideology. In this case, the Calvinist insistence on predestination has been combined with the social-Darwinist insistence on the survival of the fittest in order to create a "self-made man" mythology, combining the simultaneous worship of God and Mammon! The American fundamentalists, who hate Darwin's theory of evolution with a passion, apparently forgot that William Jennings Bryan, their champion in the 1925 "Monkey Trial", was also a lifelong foe of social-Darwinism and free enterprise.

But today's fundamentalists have long forgotten their populist origins. They have somehow managed to convince themselves that using government money to help the poor directly is evil, while using the same government money to help religious charities is a good thing. Turning elementary logic upside down, they are capable of supporting the rich and the powerful in their pork-barrel theft of the government treasury, while simultaneously denying any government role in social policy. For them, evil is good and good is evil.

The ultra-white, ultra-Christian, ultra-patriotic, ultra-Nazis, all over the Western world, firmly believe that any social justice at all is a sign of weakness and of imminent Armageddon. Apparently, in the USA, they are even capable of convincing themselves that if ever any woman or any socialist or any Jewish person should one day be elected President, God might "authorize" them to use the entire American military arsenal on the USA itself! If they ever lose hope in the ultimate victory of their antediluvian cause, they could end up destroying their own civilization, and the rest of the world with it, rather than let the USA become another Sodom and Gomorrah forever. Unfortunately, such people also exist in all the other Christian countries.

This peculiarly Christian paradox, however, is only one of many such abominations, which paradoxically include even the so-called communist movement, which promoted mass-murder, state-capitalism and the cult of the toxic personality rather than any kind of socialism. Another example comes from the radical Islamic organizations' curious combination of terrorism and social-welfare. Under the watchful eye of the mullahs and the imams, these militants thoroughly enjoy promulgating equal doses of submission to God, alms-giving and the satanic massacre of thousands of innocent civilians. If they had the power, they would kill as many unbelievers as the Christian countries have succeeded in doing.

In fact, the stupidest idea currently circulating in the world is that human beings somehow need some sort of collective religion or ideology in order to make them obey the rules. All sorts of foolish people are always crowing something to the effect that today's individualism has created a dangerous situation in society, since we are no longer ruled by

25

some kind of overpowering system of ideas which make us behave properly. In the real world, however, all of the important religions and ideologies have always been used in order to help toxic personalities evade the rules. No evildoer at any level of society has ever been deterred from harming someone else because of his or her belief in any particular religion or ideology.

In the same fashion, different kinds of societies set up at different points in history, on every continent, have always acted in similar ways. People in the so-called Third World (Asia, Africa, Latin America and Oceania) often get justifiably upset at the European colonialism of the past five centuries, when the various commercial empires from Europe took over the entire planet. In many places, millions of indigenous people were completely wiped out, more often than not deliberately. What the anti-colonial protesters often forget, however, is that if any other non-European culture had come up with the same political and technological advantages as the Europeans did, they would have destroyed Europe to the same extent that the Europeans destroyed several other continents. The proof of this contention is that most of the immoral characteristics of modern colonialism, such as chattel slavery, existed in dozens of different civilizations, at least in embryonic form, long before European expansion began.

All over the world, and in all periods of history, all of humanity's always hypocritical leaders become not only successful politicians and generals, nor only successful investors and entrepreneurs. They also become successful union leaders and religious leaders, famous and infamous artists and scientists, everyone whose own long-term lack of sufficient talent has led them to rip off those around them and then to pretend that they were "self-made". In reality, all of these VIPs depended on a whole slew of other people's efforts in order to succeed, but they all knew that successful leadership required making off with everyone else's contributions and passing off other people's work as their own.

To make things worse, the same kind of theft of other people's lives occurs on every level of society, not just at the top but right down to everybody's household, every family and every neighborhood. The toxic personalities who ruin everything all the time, like the poor, are always among us.

This is not, to say the least, a very popular interpretation of events. Most people believe that their leaders are in fact exceptionally capable individuals, whose occasional excesses are only caused by the greater importance of their function. Ordinary people like to think that those in power, at whatever level, deserve whatever perks they may receive, up to and including worldwide fame and/or numerous stock options, because of the greater responsibility that they have to bear.

However, what ordinary people fail to realize is that the toxic personalities who lead us are unaware of those responsibilities, since for them leadership is nothing more than a foolish word which covers for what they are really doing. In reality, most of these toxic personalities are simply using the glories of domination as a way of satisfying their own egos, those black holes of bottomless ambition which really motivate them. Most of them could not care less what happens to the community, or the economy, or the nation, or the faithful, or the family, so long as they remain on top. They do not in fact bear any of the responsibility that ordinary people attribute to them.

This is why most social theory is so often erroneous. People who write textbooks on philosophy, or psychology, or political science, or economics, or sociology, have a tendency to describe their fields of study in a romantic and normalizing way. They try to describe society as it ought to be rather than as it is. They talk about the father's role in the family, or the investor's role in the economy, or the statesman's role in the country, or the pastor's role in the church, as if these people were actually performing the tasks to which they are nominally assigned. Most of the time, however, people in power do not spend their days fulfilling their official assignments. They have bureaucrats and flunkeys to do whatever small amount of real work might be necessary, just to keep up appearances.

As every official transcript can attest, from the Nixon tapes right on down to the interviews that police officers and social workers are constantly recording at the neighborhood level, what is really going on most of the time is that people in power (whether at the United Nations or at the corner store) spend most of their time getting power and maneuvering others so that they can remain in power.

The toxic personality is the classic manipulator, who may be a loudmouth some of the time but is more often than not a silent Nazi, getting others to do his or her bidding without getting visibly upset most of the time. In fact, all it takes to become a toxic personality is a total disregard for the rights of others and a complete lack of any positive human emotions. Talent and true competence are sometimes present, but they are not absolutely necessary, since domination is never really based on talent. What is really important is a system of power for power's sake which puts toxic personalities on top and keeps them on top long after it has been universally established that they should really be scavenging on the bottom!

Organized fraud is at the root of toxic power. Ambitious monsters who are only interested in their own domination manage to manipulate most of the sheep around them into accepting their power, either for fear of rocking the boat or by emulation of their perceived strength. Like vampires or the horrible creatures always being invented in Hollywood movies, toxic personalities then suck their energy out of all the nice guys or gals around them, who then always finish last. Fresh, happy, talented, healthy nobodies become their indispensable victims, providing them with the life-force that they need in order to keep on surviving, long after the death of their own pre-toxic creativity.

This is why toxic personalities often create confusion among observers. As a result, two entirely contradictory judgments are often considered equally true by the experts in any field of study! For example, Concordia University historian Graeme Decarie recently wrote an article in a Montreal newspaper in which he claimed that Ronald Reagan was, at one and the same time, both a fearless defender of democracy against communism and a corrupt, anti-democratic warmonger. According to Decarie, both statements are simultaneously true, belonging to the same person in the same time span and proven by the same facts.

Decarie also added that many other historical figures can be interpreted in the same way. Another example he gave was of Richard the Lion Heart, a medieval king of England, who was at one and the same time a fearless warrior and champion of Christian Europe, as well as being a plunderer and a murderer of Moslems and of other Christians. Decarie's point was that historical data can be used to prove several opposing contentions simultaneously.

By the same token, it could be argued that even though 90% of all current investment may be speculative and for the almost exclusive benefit of the owners of stock options, the system still somehow succeeds in providing enough useful capital to keep the world economy going, at least so far. In other words, professional apologists can still claim, with a reasonable amount of credibility, that in spite of every rip-off, whether ancient or recent, all of the wars, the depressions and the famines of days gone by have not yet managed to stop the onward march of humanity, from the few hundred-thousand hunter-gatherers of the Paleolithic period to the six-billion-strong, post-industrial world of today. Naturally, this is cold comfort to the hundreds of millions of dead victims over the years, but it is very good news indeed for the toxic personalities' public relations.

From a skeptic's point of view, however, what is important to underline in this discussion is that none of the people who run the world or even the local community, and none of the institutions that maintain their power, are now or ever have been worthy of our support. The usefulness of all skeptical observations about society is that they save us from believing anyone's propaganda about anything and therefore from committing any of our precious time, effort or money to other people's causes.

People generally hate to be reminded that their world is not a particularly nice place to live in and that practical solutions to major problems simply do not exist most of the time. There is no getting around the fact that, to the extent that the world is being run by anyone, it is almost always being run by a bunch of highly incompetent egomaniacs. The greater population in today's world only means that the number of victims has increased proportionately.

Toxic personalities usually get away with manipulating others because most people conveniently get upset at those who denounce the perpetrators rather than at the evil ones themselves. Whenever some particularly horrible manipulation takes place, the whistle-blower is always punished more than the criminal manipulator, who usually gets off lightly, even in those rare cases when the manipulators are even accused or tried. Like generals fighting an unjust war, they are much less severely punished than the draft-resisters or the deserters who refused to fight.

Unfortunately, a number of very sympathetic people, who agree with the similar arguments that I also put into my first book, are nevertheless very reluctant to write or to say anything like this, because it circumvents the usual social pressures. The problem here is that most people cannot stand feeling isolated from their peer groups, even when they have to make major sacrifices in order to do so. These people therefore dismiss my arguments on the grounds that they find my work too shrill and emotional, that it is not written in a sober and reasonable manner and that it reeks of rage and moral indignation.

Guilty as charged. I myself have often read my own writing and got the impression that I could in fact be exaggerating, that things could not possibly be as bad as what I have made them out to be. After that, however, I only have to read another serious book or newspaper, or watch another in-depth news report on television, and I invariably find out that I was not exaggerating at all. In fact, more often than not, I also have a slight tendency to let the bad guys off the hook. It turns out that the world really is as bad as everything that I have been saying, if not more so!

The source of the problem is that membership in any particular peer-group causes most people to pull their punches and to avoid making unpleasant observations about anything.

Those who think that there must be some kind of solution to any problem will inevitably tone down or dilute their description of reality so as to accommodate closure. They will let sadistic leaders off the hook as much as possible in a bid to make a (fictitious) future solution more attainable. As for me, I am simply trying to avoid the same fate.

In order to avoid socially-motivated lying, description is always better than prescription. While it is true that any human description of anything is never entirely honest and value-free, those descriptions in which people try to be honest are still better than deliberate, straightforward lying and propaganda. On the contrary, a deliberate attempt to avoid leadership and prescription will inevitably result in a more accurate description of reality. As soon as anyone tries to act on anything, to change a situation in some direction or another, that person necessarily skews his "initial" description of the problem in the direction of his intended "solution".

A more or less similar problem arises when people assume that just because everyone has done any number of evil things in his or her life, this means that it is horribly self-righteous to get so upset about other people's failings. Christians like to quote something which Jesus of

Nazareth was supposed to have said, to the effect that someone who thinks about doing something wrong is just as guilty as someone who actually did something wrong.

The problem with this objection is one of degree: shoplifting is mixed up with grand larceny, while common assault is confused with murder. After all, judges in court do not normally condemn the driver of the getaway car to the same number of years in prison as the guy who shot the bank teller.

The point is that even though everyone is guilty of something, some people are guilty of a whole lot more than just something. As often happens, many people who are fully justified in expressing their moral indignation refrain from doing so out of false modesty, whereas many more people who have no right whatsoever to be indignant about anything at all do so anyway, from unjustified egoism.

Given all the different elements in human society which reek of hypocrisy and propaganda, I still feel that I am making a contribution to human life by advocating universal skepticism. In my opinion, there is no area of human endeavor in which this attitude cannot be of help. Indeed, genuine skepticism ought to go beyond the narrow limits that most skeptics have set for themselves so as to make skepticism into a truly universal approach to life.

UNIVERSAL SKEPTICISM AS A WAY OF LIFE

Since the publication of my first book, I have also become increasingly aware of all those other people who have made it their goal in life to promote the skeptical approach toward human problems. The USA, for example, is particularly fortunate in having many thousands of scientists and other scientifically-minded individuals who write for, edit and publish several different magazines dedicated to skepticism. The organizations that promote these magazines are particularly interested in debunking the claims of all sorts of fools and charlatans who are constantly regurgitating tired old stories of magic concerning UFOs (Unidentified Flying Objects) and ETs (extra-terrestrials). The best skeptics are also attempting to rid the world of religious charlatanism as well, with its sundry gods and seventh-day creationists, not to mention genocidal racists, universal conspiracy theorists, anti-Semites and so on.

The efforts of these skeptics are all highly commendable endeavors, similar to those of the various humanist, atheist and ethical-union organizations who do like-minded work. I have no interest whatsoever in downplaying or depreciating any of the first-rate contributions that all of these people are making to twenty-first-century civilization. In today's world, religion has become the primary source of barbarian behavior, in which a highly-organized, secular society is being attacked by religious totalitarians beset by feelings of inadequacy. It is entirely true that dark, totalitarian religions and ideologies have once again become every bright, civilized person's worst enemy.

In my opinion, the only problem with the secular skeptics' current efforts is the public limitations that they have so far placed on the usefulness of skepticism. Instead of just taking on such three-letter abominations as U-F-O and G-O-D, I feel that they should also be tackling such other three-letter combinations as U-S-A, not to mention a particularly obnoxious, six-letter animal known as N-E-O-C-O-N.

In other words, skepticism as a method should not just be confined to debunking magic, pseudo-science and religion; it should also help us out with our understanding of politics, economics and society in general. For example, the number-one attack on scientific thinking nowadays, since the events of September 11, 2001, is the contention that "We are all Americans now", as well as the Western gunslinger slogan according to which "You are either for us, or against us". The same attitude was evident during the 2003 invasion of Iraq and several other recent events.

From the point of view of ordinary scientific skepticism, those statements are as off-the-wall as any story about little green men from Roswell, New Mexico (1947), or even the famous line from the 1925 Scopes trial concerning the Biblical origins of Lot's wife. Nothing about the terrorist attacks on the USA can justify any attempt to equate American patriotism with civilization itself, any more than the Nazi attacks on the USSR back in the 1940s should have turned everyone in the world into a bunch of Communist sympathizers. Throughout history, and particularly in recent times, all sorts of different people have been attacked in all sorts of heinous ways, and millions of people have died, violently and prematurely, all over the world. None of those attacks meant that the people watching them should automatically support whatever cause that the unfortunate victims were supposed to be upholding at the time that they were killed.

If we want to understand the USA or any other country as it really is, and to understand dictators and the various terrorist groups for what they really are, then we have to put aside any parochial attitudes toward human conflict. What happened on September 11, 2001, for example, was not all that different from what has happened in a whole lot of other places, before and since. In that particular event, all that happened (very dramatically, of course) was that a small group of Moslem extremists successfully carried out an especially murderous attack on urban civilians in the USA.

The number of people killed was incredibly high for that kind of operation, but it was nowhere near as high as the number of civilian victims caused by hundreds of other well-planned killing sprees throughout human history. Even in the USA, the number of deaths in the 2001 event, although it was definitely higher than the Oklahoma City murders, was still a lot fewer than those caused by, say, General Sherman's march through Georgia during the Civil War, or even the 1877 railroad strike in and around Pennsylvania. In fact, the main difference between the September 11, 2001, attack, and other cases of mass murder of civilians in the USA, was that it was so much more rapid.

Of course, the impact on North America was much sharper in 2001 than it was for similar events either taking place in this part of the world several decades ago, or even some of the events taking place more recently, but in other parts of the world. Since the Second World War, most people in the Western world have not had to contend with death on that scale, at least not in their own back yards. Nor were past events, or even most contemporary events in other countries, instantly televised in such a spectacular fashion.

Still, none of that justifies applying any "American exceptionalism" to the terrorist attacks on New York, Washington and Pennsylvania. The retaliatory bombing of civilians in Afghanistan may have been an understandable reaction to those events, at least from a geopolitical point of view, regardless of whether or not those bombs succeeded in killing the same number of innocent victims as were killed in the USA. But that bombing was not necessarily more civilized.

Nor was the idea of starting a second war on Iraq. All sorts of foolish people have argued that invading Iraq in 2003 was supposed to be part of the war on terrorism, but the real effect of that event was simply to increase the chances of new attacks of the 9/11 type. In fact, supporting the war on Iraq was as foolish as was supporting Saddam Hussein, since both those options only served to intensify conflict and to justify ongoing military action on both sides.

This ties in quite well with many observers' contention that the justification for the 2003 attack on Iraq was not any link between Hussein's national-socialism and Islamic fundamentalism. It was indeed caused by geopolitical considerations, such as the need for the USA and Great Britain to wrest control of Iraq's petroleum away from rival interests. Also involved was a desire to use a new Iraqi puppet regime as a comprador neo-colony in the heart of Western Asia, sandwiching theocratic Iran in between American-occupied Iraq and American-occupied Afghanistan. Last but not least, it was also a good way to provide coalition armies with on-the-job training so that they do not become too bored, as well as to justify the enormous military expenditures of the nations involved.

The same type of reasoning should also be used when referring to the still-ongoing war between the Israeli army and the Palestinian terrorist organizations: the deaths inflicted on the one side are highly understandable, but they do not in any way justify the deaths inflicted on the other side. All of these conflicts have simply become self-sustaining monstrosities, so that both sides can go on fighting forever, before, during and after all the endless attempts at making peace. The same kind of observations also applies to the never-ending conflict between the Chechens and the Russian empire.

The whole point is that taking sides in any such situation is useless, and always takes the observer as far away from the truth as it is possible to go. In the case of the USA's war on Moslem terrorism, it does no good whatsoever to, on the one hand, become an American patriot, or on the other hand, become an anti-American propagandist. With George W. Bush and Tony Blair on one side, with Noam Chomsky and Susan Sontag on the other, none of us are any closer to understanding what is really going on.

The same reasoning should also be applied to the debate between the war hawks in the USA, Britain and Australia, who are still trying to set up a new colony in Iraq, and the peaceniks in Europe who wanted the United Nations to save Saddam Hussein. As in any other geopolitical situation, none of the countries involved really supported whatever it was they say they supported for any of the officially stated reasons. The USA, France, Germany, Russia, and China, even Iraq itself: all of these countries always have underlying economic and geopolitical reasons for taking whatever position that they take. Mere regime changes never make ordinary geopolitics go away; only the rhetoric ever really changes all that much.

People should also stop believing in the official shibboleth according to which local wars can all be started, controlled and successfully stopped without any danger of world war. The various combinations of powers which exist nowadays and the multi-polar concentrations of weapons of mass destruction make a world conflagration every bit as possible as it used to be during the Cold War. Nuclear weapons in particular are not as well protected by relatively rational governments as they once were. Skepticism about official reasons for doing things, and about the rationality of today's actors, is as justified nowadays as it ever was.

Instead of repeating someone else's opinion about motives, we should always adopt an attitude of universal skepticism, now as in the past. As in any other scientific investigation, this does not necessarily mean that we will inevitably end up as far away from one side's point of view as from the other side's point of view. What it does mean is that it is totally impossible to arrive at a satisfactory conclusion if we start out with garbage slogans like "May my country always be right, but my country right or wrong."

All the other political disputes currently going on, large or small, local or global, should be approached in exactly the same skeptical way. Consider for example the seemingly endless fight between Canadian federalism and the Quebec independence movement. Even though this is a much less murderous example than the wars referred to earlier, it is still another case in point, since the nationalism of one group is not necessarily better or worse than the nationalism of the other group.

During one of the more entertaining wrinkles in the Canadian constitutional debate, back in 1981, the federalist politicians from Quebec all voted in favor of a new Canadian constitution which made it harder for Quebec separation to take place legally. As a result, the separatist organizations accused the federalist politicians of being "traitors" to the Quebec nation. The federalist politicians then retaliated by taking the separatists to court, demanding millions of dollars in damages for alleged rhetorical excess.

After over twenty years of deliberations, the Canadian court system finally rendered its decision: while the accusation of treachery was declared excessive, damages were refused since in a democracy people have the right to exaggerate. In reality, however, the judges were wrong about the alleged excess. The federalist politicians were undoubtedly acting as traitors to the Quebec nation, but only because they were simultaneously acting as patriots to the Canadian nation. By the same token, the Quebec separatists were and are traitors to the Canadian nation simply because they have always been patriots for the Quebec nation.

It was the taking of sides which led both groups into an interpretative dead-end. Nationalism will still be nationalism no matter which constitutional option wins the debate, and politics will still be politics. None of the sides involved is particularly interested in knowing that no one gang has any predetermined moral advantage over the other gang. This applies as much to the wars in the Middle East as it does to Canada's constitution, or to any other human conflict.

On yet another level of debate, this would also seem to be one of the main reasons why some people continue to believe in God, rather than to accept the fact that no evidence for the existence of any god has ever been found. Even though a lot of people like to think that religious debates are not at all related to geopolitical debates, in fact they are controlled by the same underlying, psychological impulses. Most people go through life being pushed around by all sorts of physical, biological and sociological forces over which they have no control whatsoever. To counter their feelings of helplessness and impotence, some of those people decide to deny reason and to have faith instead. Their faith then allows them to fuse themselves with an imagined, omnipotent force that allows them to vicariously control the entire universe.

A gang of people doing this sort of thing together can then collectively invent the illusion that their way of seeing things is better than anyone else's way of seeing things. With God on their side, this allows them to believe that their political choices (Bush or Bin Laden, Israel or Palestine, Quebec or Canada, etc.) automatically become better choices than the other side's choice. By eliminating their collective impotence and allowing them to "win" all of their political debates, belief in God provides them with the ultimate power trip. It is no coincidence that the greatest concentrations of Christian fundamentalists are in the USA, Britain and Australia, precisely the three countries most involved in the 2003 invasion of Iraq. Not to mention their common support for Israel; that is at least until the Armageddon dreamed up by the feverish brains of the fundamentalists comes along and what is left of the world's Jews will presumably have to convert to Christianity just like everyone else or be blown to smithereens!

Having God or righteousness on their side also allows religious people to theoretically get away with heinous crimes for which people motivated only by secular ideologies are supposed to be punished. In this way, religious motivation was said to have justified the attacks of the Crusaders of the Middle Ages on rival Christians and Jews as well as on the Moslem enemy. Modern-day crusaders use similar arguments, as when seventh-day Adventists used religion to justify their participation in many of the recent civil wars and attempted genocides in Africa. Religion was also invoked to justify all-out Pentecostal support for right-wing dictatorships in Latin America during the Cold War, dictatorships which had even been denounced by some of the conservative bishops in the Catholic Church.

The most ardent believers are even capable of invoking God in an Old Testament (Talmudic) fashion, by pretending that divine intervention into human affairs is a daily occurrence. They interpret things like the September 11, 2001 attacks as God's punishment to Americans for daring to remove religion from school pledges. Some of them even go so far as to claim that God told them which person they ought to marry. They avoid all personal responsibility for their actions by blaming every ignorant decision on the Supreme Being, their slogan being "My life is not my own". Even otherwise intelligent adults are capable of acting like children when it comes to religion.

Unfortunately for such believers, their whole house of cards comes crashing down with the first breath of reason. For one thing, believers have to admit that God is impotent rather than all-powerful, since he created both the sinners and their victims on this planet, thereby letting his own people get mistreated all the time by the other side. No ignorant posturing about free will can possibly erase the fact that the creator obviously did not know what he was doing when he made this world. Why not just create a perfect universe in the first place rather than play around in this ridiculous manner? If people turned out wrong, why not just start over and make them right? Good and evil cannot co-exist with total power on one side. Biological evolution and human history, with all of their obvious imperfections, are further proofs of the non-existence of God. In the long run, the only ideal universe is nothingness.

Similarly, God cannot possibly support every individual's conflicting choices, nor support both sides in every dispute, since there are believers claiming divine intervention on every side of every debate. With or without a supreme being, the personal wishes or the proselytizing efforts of one point of view are always canceling out the personal wishes or the proselytizing efforts of the opposing point of view. One choice of spouse over another, government intervention versus free enterprise, Christianity versus Islam, the USA versus the rest of the world, federalism versus independence; nobody ever gets ahead in any of these debates since there are so many true believers on every side.

This is why the oath which is apparently used in some American courts is so misleading. People are supposed to put their hand on the Bible, a book full of dozens of rather obvious contradictions, and say, "I swear to tell the truth, the whole truth and nothing but the truth, so help me God". The part about telling the truth is fine, but the entire ceremony is ruined by the presence of the religious book and by the reference to God, since monotheist religion has turned out to be the biggest lie ever invented. No self-respecting supreme being would ever want to be in the uncomfortable position of being worshipped in such hypocritical ways.

I suggest therefore that our goal in all of these debates should be to do away with all such crutches and to use universal skepticism as a tool to free ourselves as much as is humanly possible from any of the prejudices associated with political, economic, social and cultural activity on this planet. Magic and religion are important enemies of rational thought, but not any more so than any of the world's other ideologies.

As I pointed out earlier in my first book, our main goal has to be to do away with all forms of group-behavior, or parochialism, in every country and in every walk of life. Parochialism is a major problem not just in smaller, less powerful countries like Laos or Liberia, but also in larger, more powerful countries like China and the USA. This latter country is particularly paradoxical in this regard.

On the one hand, it is easily the country which depends the most on the importation of both natural and human resources from all over the world, including a very high proportion of foreign capital to finance growing deficits. On the other hand, among the richer countries at least, it is also the one whose population has the most insular, protectionist and self-sufficient attitude. The inherent hypocrisy of the USA is the most obvious in the entire world, since its perceived strength allows it to get away with refusing to apply any international protocols of behavior to itself, while still expecting other countries to comply with them. American exceptionalism has become American unilateralism.

This kind of parochialism, in which the world's only superpower acts like it was a small village, also applies almost as much to the rest of the world's people as it does to the USA. In fact, that country is more to blame only because it is so much more powerful than any of the others and not because Americans are inherently more small-minded than other people. Parochialism is humanity's most important problem everywhere, not only in world politics, which I will return to later, but also in the more mundane aspects of life.

DOMESTICATED HUMANS

One of the more disgusting problems that civilized people have had to put up with over the years is the obsession that many of our fellow humans have with pets. From somewhere within the reptilian section of their brains, perhaps left over from their barbarian childhood, a relatively large number of people seem to find that their lives would be incomplete without burdening themselves, and their neighbors, with some sort of domesticated animal. The origin of this disease may have something to do with primitive hunting and fishing, or with myths having to do with shepherds and cowboys. What is certain is that none of these pet species have any business living in a modern city, and should be confined instead to the countryside.

Some homegrown animals are less damaging to the urban environment than others. While it may not be very nice to keep small fish or small birds inside various types of cages, their effect on other people living in the same neighborhood is not usually all that great. Sometimes, bigger domesticated animals can be a lot more dangerous, such as alligators and iguanas, but the number of such abominations is still relatively limited. The real problem comes with the much more popular, but still too large animals, such as cats and dogs.

As for the cat, far too many millions of these unfortunate creatures are kept cooped up in various houses and apartments, where their primary purpose has long since ceased to be the capture of small rodents. While most of them are intelligent enough to at least cover their digestive wastes with whatever product is provided for that purpose, the resultant odors are still obvious to any and all visitors. Cat noises are often abominable,

41

however, as are the traces left behind by those felines whose owners have not bothered to alter their sexual natures. Dogs, however, are much worse.

Nothing is more ridiculous than to watch some domesticated human trotting out along a sidewalk, waiting for his or her dog to do his or her business in public. If properly trained, the human will then scoop up the remains of the animal's defecation, shovel it into a bag and take it home for proper disposal. Untrained humans, however, often let their pets pollute the urban environment, in which case the offending substance ultimately becomes the property of the city sanitation department, after having spent a couple of disgusting weeks being avoided by hundreds of innocent pedestrians.

Even if the leftovers are properly removed, however, the public defecation process is still abominable. No city dweller should be forced to watch other people's animals doing their business on a public thoroughfare. Animal defecation, and urination, should be banned from the urban public in the same way that similar human activity is also banned.

This kind of primitive behavior must be particularly damaging to really young children, whose toilet training is most certainly disrupted by excessive adult tolerance of animals. It must put a lot of stress on a really young psyche to realize that he, or she, is not permitted to do what other animals are so benevolently encouraged to accomplish.

In a world with over six billion people, most of them now living in cities, owners of property have to become responsible for their possessions. Homeowners and apartment dwellers have to take care of their garbage, just like commercial and industrial proprietors should be obliged to take care of their pollution. Everyone should be required to deal with the consequences of his or her own deeds and activities. The same thing should apply to dog owners: they should be forced to treat their pet's biological processes as if these were their own biological processes, or those of their children.

Unfortunately, the problem with dogs is much larger than mere urination and defecation. In most neighborhoods, dogs also make a great deal of noise. Almost every neighborhood possesses at least one dog owner who lets his animal yap at every single moving object, at all times of day or night, sometimes for hours on end. Those individuals should have their pets removed and put out of their misery, either by being moved to the countryside where they belong or by being otherwise eliminated in the most humane manner possible.

Dogs which bite should be dealt with immediately, particularly the kind of attack dog which several pro-fascist city dwellers insist on keeping around the house. Attack dogs are a lot like guns since they normally belong to people whose fear of the dark makes them exceptionally ignorant. In at least half of all violent incidents, the gun or the dog eventually end up being used against the owner's own people.

The main character in the 1997 American film, "As Good As It Gets", received a lot of laughs by throwing one particularly obnoxious pet down the garbage chute in a big-city apartment. Of course, to placate dog owners in the USA, this same character was eventually punished for what he did. The idea of throwing the offending animal in the garbage is not, however, really practical, no more than the even better idea of throwing its owner into the same chute. What should really happen is that people who let their property significantly worsen other people's daily lives should be forced to pay a fine, or be sent to jail, just like any other small-time criminal.

Charles Danten, an ex-veterinarian who recently published an article on pets in a Montreal newspaper, has pointed out that humans with pets do not even keep them for love and affection, but in fact to demonstrate domination and to build ego. None of the pets are ever as well treated as they are supposed to be, whereas even the animal-rights activists are not at all genuinely interested in the animals' welfare. Like Mother Teresa, they really enjoy acting like saints and getting high off of protecting creatures that no one else wants to protect. Most pets are in fact treated like just any other material commodity, to be bought and sold, "altered" and killed, loved and protected, cherished and abandoned, according to the selfish whims of their owners.

Another galling aspect of this problem is the sums of money involved. Billions of dollars are spent every year on these unfortunate creatures, which could be used in at least a thousand better ways. Millions of human lives could be significantly improved, not only by getting rid of pets but also by spending those sums on the health, education and welfare of human beings, the three aspects of life which have been most neglected since the "conservative revolution" of the 1980s.

Instead, we have all of those strange people out there, some of whom at least materially treat their pets far better than they treat other people, often including their own children. In the richer countries, the court systems have even begun handing out stiffer penalties to people who mistreat animals than to those who mistreat other humans. In a relatively recent case, a man was sentenced to three years in jail for throwing a particularly photogenic animal into ongoing traffic. Anyone who follows the news knows that thousands of drunk drivers, informers and other criminals received much lighter sentences than that for the killing of their fellow humans.

The contemporary attitude toward animals, particularly in the Western world, is increasingly inconsistent. Wild animals, farm animals and pets are all treated differently, not only as overall categories but also according to all sorts of even more foolish criteria. An animal's look, whether as a species or as an individual, usually determines its treatment: cute and cuddly results in lavish care, whereas ugly and scaly brings out the army. This kind of differential treatment cannot even be traced to the animal's place on the evolutionary scale. Even proximity to humans is no longer considered important.

The poorer countries are even more afflicted by this problem, as usual, than are the richer countries. In India, the situation is particularly insane, with hundreds of millions of human beings allowing themselves to remain in exceptional poverty, while tolerating the equally miserable existence of millions of religiously sanctioned animals, even in built-up areas. The Chinese attitude toward dogs is exemplary, since they are treated as a major nuisance. However, the Eastern Asian habit of killing off millions of animals for their phallic symbols is not particularly edifying. As with most Third World problems, this one does not seem to be headed toward any kind of solution.

Unfortunately, the pet situation even in the richer countries is not going to change for the better any time soon. The most that we can hope for is that the progressive replacement of human brain cells by more efficient electronic chips, over the next few decades, will eventually wipe out the antediluvian urge to keep these animals around the house forever.

THE NO FAULT SOCIETY

In my first book, I made a brief reference to the concept of a no fault society in the chapter on discrimination. The no fault society simply refers to another one of those absurd tendencies that make contemporary life more difficult than it has any right to be. Millions of people seem to enjoy encouraging each other to avoid any kind of responsibility for their actions.

One of the most infuriating examples of that is a law that was passed in the province of Quebec back in 1978, setting up a public automobile insurance system. Under this system, all of the people involved in car accidents are compensated for any losses they may have sustained. They are paid by a government-controlled fund, without any regard whatsoever as to their degree of guilt in causing the accident. Innocent passengers and bystanders are awarded sums equal to those given to drunk drivers and various other criminal elements. According to this system, an accident is just that, which is to say nobody's fault.

No great deal of intelligence is required to figure out that this program does not discourage people from driving recklessly, particularly since the government so far prohibits victims from taking the bad guys to court. As long as this system continues to operate, there is simply no way to make anyone pay for any of the crimes regularly committed, no matter how outrageous the particular circumstances might have been. A worthless justification for this approach is the argument about most reckless drivers being insolvent and therefore unable to pay fines if found guilty, since criminals can always be jailed instead.

The current government of that province has recently decided to find a more appropriate solution, but it remains to be seen if the new system will work any better. The whole point of any changes ought to be forcing toxic drivers to pay for their crimes in one way or another without requiring the rest of the population to cover for their stupidity. Behaving like private insurance companies, by increasing everyone's premiums in order to compensate for a few thousand repeat offenders, is equally insane.

Some way should be found so that irresponsible drivers can be sued, or jailed, without penalizing innocent people. The last thing that ought to be encouraged is the kind of frivolous lawsuits currently afflicting North American society, in which people with some sort of nasty habit or another are trying to blame companies or governments for "forcing" them to consume some disgusting substance. Using this kind of logic, even ordinary criminals could just as easily sue police forces for putting them in jail, since there are any number of Ph. D. theses in sociology available for study which could be used to prove, at least statistically, that millions of people having committed the same crimes as all prison inmates have committed, have not so far been arrested.

Gambling, obesity and nicotine addiction are a lot like road accidents: very few accidents really take place without anyone ever having been guilty of anything. The Quebec system of car insurance still currently treats the entire population of the province, about seven million people altogether, as one unit, which is then taxed to provide a fund for dealing with accidents. Once again, if the same method were to be adopted in the criminal justice system, this would mean that no one would ever be charged for anything, let alone punished. Everyone would simply pitch in and pay equally for everything, as if all human beings were equally responsible for every crime committed!

Unfortunately, this is exactly what takes place most of the time anyway, since very few criminals are ever punished to the full extent of the law. The same type of thing also happens with pet owners, as I pointed in the preceding chapter. Industrial pollution, false advertising, insider trading, proxy wars, civilians being used as military targets—the list is simply endless of rotten things that people do to each other without any suitable punishment ever being handed out.

The same ridiculous attitude is also adopted towards the anti-social behavior of youth gangs in the world's various ghettoes. Graffiti,

46

vandalism, bullying, taxing, aggravated assault, violent robbery and so on are among the kinds of behavior often tolerated, if not even encouraged, as long as it is being carried out by some kind of local minority. Social discrimination is somehow supposed to justify this kind of thing, which people assume is caused by the breakdown of social institutions like religion or patriotism or civic pride. In fact, however, this so-called individualism is just another form of local tribalism, with "underprivileged" youth gangs imitating the kind of anti-social behavior which is common among lawyers, investors, political leaders and other toxic personalities.

Each one of these immoral events is the result of some particular faulty process. In the case of the still-current Quebec automobile insurance scheme, the reasons for setting it up in the first place were actually quite good. Before 1978, thousands of people had their lives ruined by a group of lawyers and shylocks, who made millions of dollars off of the victims' misery, in a totally unregulated insurance industry.

The same free-for-all still characterizes most private-insurance schemes elsewhere, such as in most parts of the USA. Social justice is certainly not greater in a country or a region which encourages lawyers to charge whatever fees they may, and that always results in those people winning who have that much more money to spend. In the USA, for example, O. J. Simpson proved just how free rich Blacks had become by pulling off the same kind of financial manipulation of the court system that rich Whites used to monopolize. In fact, the free-enterprise system is no improvement whatsoever over Quebec's socialist car insurance. Victims of alcohol-soaked drivers are not any better off if they also become the victims of greed-soaked lawyers.

It turns out that neither the socialist nor the free-enterprise "solution" to the problem in fact guarantees responsible behavior. Preventing one group from ruining other people's lives with their cars does not justify letting another group ruin other people's lives with endless, overpriced litigation. People are always relying on competing ideologies to provide either an individualist or a collectivist illusion of justice. In fact, real justice has nothing to do with either approach, since real justice can always be postulated but it has so far never been witnessed in the real world.

47

The same kind of observation about no-fault insurance has also been made about industrial or agricultural pollution, not to mention automobile emissions and power-plant effluents. It is a still very rare event for any of the individuals, companies or governments running any of humanity's numerous plants or machines to be forced to pay the full price for ruining everyone else's environment. Almost none of these groups are ever obliged to use most of the anti-pollution technologies already available, nor to pay for developing new ones. So far as the private automobile is concerned, making every driver pay, as some have suggested, through higher gasoline taxes, has the same built-in defect, since it still does not differentiate between the more-guilty and the less-guilty.

Meanwhile, the debate still rages over smoking, with big tobacco companies getting away with organizing massive tax-evasion schemes and individual smokers getting away with killing others through second-hand smoke in places where people congregate. Nothing is more ridiculous than to watch all sorts of people knowingly harm themselves, and everyone else, by refusing to quit smoking. Particularly nauseating are the "progressive" smokers, people whose all-out participation in the ecology movement or on behalf of some other socially worthy cause should have prevented them from smoking—but never does. Marijuana, by the way, is not any less harmful than nicotine.

All over the world, all sorts of private citizens, companies, armies and other government agencies dump hazardous wastes all over the place, including Antarctica and outer space, normally without being obliged to clean up after themselves. Compensation for past misdeeds sometimes takes place in extreme cases, such as the sums paid by Germany to Israel for the murder of several million European Jews, even though the amounts are most often paid to the wrong people. In the meantime, however, new crimes are committed all the time without any thought of present or future redress.

As I underlined in my first book, the majority of criminals in society are never arrested for their crimes, those arrested are not convicted nearly often enough, while those actually convicted are very seldom punished to anywhere near the extent of the damage that they caused to others. This is especially true for those criminals who happen to be Very Important Persons (VIPs): politicians, business leaders and all the other toxic personalities.

This problem has been particularly aggravated in recent years by the rise of the political correctness movement, rooted in the Western countries. In centuries gone by, as well as nowadays in many non-Western countries (which seems to include Texas, of all places), the old ways prevailed. That meant that even though VIPs were always and forever exempt from punishment, regardless of what they did, the same did not apply to ordinary (i.e., powerless) people. Slaves, serfs and workers quite often used to be punished much more than any of them ever deserved, and this sort of thing is still going on, notably in most parts of the Third World. Unfortunately, in those countries or parts of countries now under the control of political correctness, tolerance of criminal acts has been democratized. In most regions of most Western countries nowadays, even ordinary criminals are no longer getting any of the punishment which most of them so richly deserve.

Political correctness also seems to be responsible for the extremely stupid decision made in several different countries during the 1970s, to let most of the patients out of the mental hospitals so that they could spend their lives wandering around on the streets instead. The authorities apparently decided to let hundreds of thousands of sick people "rot in their rights" by opening most of the doors in dozens of different asylums, and then refusing to provide the type of community services which were supposed to take up the slack. As a result, not a day goes by without some mental patients harming either themselves or any number of unsuspecting passers-by, in a world-wide orgy of no-fault irresponsibility.

All over the world, human society seems incapable of finding a proper balance between crime and punishment. Big shots still almost always get away with everything, as was obvious once again during the most recent presidential elections in France. Ordinary criminals are now faced with a double standard: in most countries, many of them are still being punished too much, while in the most "enlightened" countries, or parts of countries, many of them are not being punished enough.

So far as insufficient punishment is concerned, the problem probably begins in childhood. Parents who were mistreated during their own upbringing often over-react and use unconditional love of children as an excuse for mollycoddling. Unconditional love, totally unrelated to behavior, is perfectly appropriate for one and two-year-old children, who naturally act like lone wolves. It starts becoming a problem, however, for children between three and seven years of age, who, in theory, should gradually be weaned away from total selfishness and introduced to the notion of other people's rights. After the age of reason, usually at age seven, inappropriate behavior should no longer be tolerated. Unfortunately, many parents are unable to get anywhere close to a reasonable standard, and end up either excessively over-punishing or excessively under-punishing.

Millions of children and adolescents, as well as millions of adults in child-like circumstances, such as many students, prison inmates, mental patients and so on, often act and react seemingly without any knowledge of the real world. The responsible people who are supposed to take care of them and to minister to their needs toil on and on for years without ever getting any recognition for their work. Dependent people often have no concept of their benefactors except as inanimate objects which do not really belong to their imagined worlds. Responsible people are often treated like beings of no consequence, for which dependent people have no deference and no respect.

In a no-fault society, all that the dependent people most often feel toward their benefactors is contempt, as if the responsible people were only getting in the way all the time and even daring to criticize their dependents' irresponsible behavior once in awhile. When this happens, the dependent groups look upon the responsible persons from a totally different cognitive point of view, much in the way that humans see extraterrestrials in the movies, or the way that Europeans looked down upon native peoples in colonial times. The dependent ones are not at all impressed by anything which the responsible ones do for them, they ignore all the money spent, all the time invested, all the work accomplished. They see the "grown-ups" as aliens and they have no sense of gratitude whatsoever.

Immature people, whether as older children or as irresponsible adults, often claim that they feel some sort of genuine emotions toward their care-givers. They claim that they respect their father or that they love their mother, or whatever other responsible person acts "in loco parentis", but in reality all such emotions are bogus. If they really respected or loved the people trying to help them, they would make an effort to stop whatever inappropriate behavior that they happen to be engaged in and at least try to function properly. Instead, they go on refusing to cooperate and continue to act irresponsibly as if total dependence and contempt for others were fundamental human rights. Often enough, they even claim to respect the law or the existence of rules in general, but only on the hypocritical condition that they do not have to obey any particular law or rule!

Students in the no-fault society cannot comprehend why they could possibly be receiving bad marks, even when they do everything wrong, often on purpose. They cannot understand a society which would restrict their access to high-paying jobs just because they did absolutely nothing to deserve them. Like all of the other under-achievers, they do not at all understand the concept of merit. They live in a no-fault society inside their own heads, in which all behavior is condoned equally and all people are equally rewarded or punished regardless of results or effort.

Criminals do not understand why they are being punished, since all that they did was to try to take a short-cut to success. They are as convinced as the other dependent people that the world owes them a living, and a superior one at that. Similar mental processes lead dictators to keep foreign aid and investment for themselves, lead farmers in famine zones to stop sowing and to rely on foreign grain shipments instead, and lead professional minority leaders to lobby for endlessly repeated government handouts rather than trying to put an end to discrimination on a long-term basis.

All of these professional dependents do not understand work, but they do understand manipulation, maneuvering, defrauding and temporary advantage. They are good at cat-fighting and baring fangs, as well as at jumping ahead of other people in line, but they cannot comprehend sustained effort or the bearing of casualties, or looking to the future with some sort of long-term plan of action. They are like Celtic warriors fighting bravely but stupidly against an organized Roman onslaught, with individual posturing as their only weapon. They cannot conceive of any of the fundamental forces and rules that produce society as a whole, or the type of cooperation which forms the underlying base upholding everything superficial.

Their whole universe is immediate and immanent, their concentration spans are limited to five or ten minutes and they hate anything or anyone who suggests something different. They have no sense of right, or devotion, or responsibility, or respect for others. They exist only for one moment's entertainment to be replaced by another, in unending succession forever, with death never intervening. Nothing which is required so that entertainment can be brought to them is real in their eyes; everything which is underlying and basic is part of an alien and foreboding universe, to be ignored for all eternity.

The result of all this is the absence of any sort of meritocracy, anywhere in the world. Real merit is almost always passed over in favor of laissez-faire image-making, as if stock manipulation were the world's most important activity. Most people let the toxic personalities who run the world get away with the idea that merit has something to do with maximizing profit or with wielding political power, rather than with making real contributions to social or cultural development.

As a result, leaders are never punished for anything, at least while they are still being active leaders. Ordinary (powerless) people are getting away with murder in some countries, while still being murdered by the state, often for no good reason, in many other countries. Very few people end up getting treated in the way that they deserve to be treated.

One of the more glaring examples of that concerns the debate over the death penalty. In some parts of the USA, for example, psychiatrists are sometimes called in to "cure" certain criminals of their mental illness, so that they can be properly executed later on! The reasoning for this foolishness seems to be that the criminal cannot be counted on to repent for his sins if he is not fully aware of the reasons why he is being punished.

In cases of this sort, society is simply calling upon professionals, such as psychiatrists, to pervert their own professions. Any doctor or psychiatrist who prolongs or intensifies his patients' suffering is like a parent who rapes his own child, or a scientist who uses his theories and discoveries to promote magic or religion.

The most absurd aspect of this particular abomination is that the people involved seem to believe that being executed is worse than life imprisonment, which is also used as an argument by those who refuse to condone capital punishment. Unfortunately, the very opposite is true. Living for a long period of time in a very confined space with all sorts of social misfits and homosexual rapists has to be a lot worse than being put out of one's misery altogether. Living on this planet, "black as the pit from pole to pole" (W. E. Henley), is bad enough, without adding metal bars and anal simians to it.

Think about it: the worst nightmare any human being could have is to be obliged to relive his or her entire life from even a few months back, knowing what was going to happen at each point and being unable to change anything at all which took place between that event and the present time. The world as it is presently constituted and our own roles in that world are not often sources for unbounded pride or contentment. If they are not psychotic, people who are confined to jail for long periods of time are being tortured every day by having to reflect over and over again on the stupidity of all of their past activities and not just the ones which landed them in prison.

This is true even for people whose current lives are relatively satisfying and who have attained the ultimate goal of the good life, which means that they have a useful job which also allows them sufficient time, money and opportunity to practice whatever scientific or cultural hobby that fascinates them most. Unfortunately, there are still very few people who can indulge in life in the way that I have by, for example, teaching history while still finding the time to publish and to market books on skepticism. But even for other people just as blessed as I am or more so, the repetition of their past lives would still constitute the ultimate punishment. A no-fault society is just a place in which people are encouraged to deny their own personal nightmares, no matter how real.

SECTARIAN STUPIDITIES

Anyone who has ever had any first-hand experience with one of the world's extremist sects, whether the religious kind or the political kind, knows what damage they can cause, to both the individuals involved and to the surrounding society. Unflinching adhesion to any one of the insane ideologies that govern these sects can lead people into doing all sorts of things that they live to regret for decades afterwards. I already denounced many of those religions and ideologies in my first book. In this chapter, I would like to present some of that first-hand experience to which I refer.

A lot of baby-boomers brought up in the 1950s entered the 1960s and the 1970s in a rebellious mood. Some of them took the hippy route, promoting the sort of "sex, drugs and rock 'n' roll" profile that has been described in tens of thousands of different books and magazines. Some of them also lost their minds in various weird religious cults, while others were sucked into the ultra-right-wing, ultra-patriotic vacuum cleaner for the brain.

As a teenager in the 1960s, with the Vietnam War underway, I got involved instead with millions of other people in the peace movement, thereby starting a twenty-five year period of political activity. The first organization I joined was a New-Left outfit called the Student Union for Peace Action in Toronto, one of a number of like-minded groups which quite rightly denounced the USA as the number-one warmonger in the world, but let all the lesser warmongers off the hook.

With that mind-set, in 1965 and 1966 I went to a series of summer conferences organized by a group of Quaker pacifists, at the Grindstone Island center in eastern Ontario. There, I found out that those pacifists had been trying to do what they called peace research by dividing their own people into opposing groups and trying to replicate the kind of social divisions and geopolitical situations which led world leaders into starting wars. Interestingly enough, the pacifists themselves ended up practically trying to kill each other in these simulations, and were no more capable of avoiding warlike behavior than world politicians were!

Like a lot of other people in these movements, I then became convinced that war was unavoidable in many circumstances, such as in Vietnam, where the communists were presumably justified in fighting for independence and social justice. This sort of one-sided thinking led me and thousands of other like-minded people into believing that we could make the whole world into a much better place for everyone by becoming communists ourselves. In fact, we ended up making it worse.

In North America and Western Europe, some of us who drifted into the New Left movement got fed up with just demonstrating against the war and decided instead to go all out and embrace the entire communist ideology. All of us ultra-radicals even tried to become more communist than the official Communist Parties who used to follow the Moscow line. We ultras therefore called those original communists, "revisionists", and instead followed either the ultra-communist teachings of the founder of the Red Army, Leon Trotsky, or the idiotic ruminations of the even more murderous Mao Zedong.

On a personal level here in Canada, my next sectarian stupidity was called the Progressive Workers' Movement, or PWM, which existed throughout the rebellious decade of 1965-1975. This was a tiny Maoist organization originally started up in Vancouver by a half-dozen former Communist Party of Canada members. Unlike most of the other ultra-communists of that period, those people had at least spent most of their lives working in factories and other such difficult places.

The Toronto branch, however, was much more like other such groups in being composed almost entirely of young, middle-class people gravitating around the universities. At one point, our little group of (at most) twenty or thirty stalwarts was raided by a somewhat larger American organization called the Progressive Labor Party (PLP). The Toronto group then left the PWM and decided to affiliate to the PLP by calling itself the

Canadian Party of Labor (CPL), presumably in imitation of the governing political party in communist Albania.

Just by being Maoist, of course, these groups were doing more harm than good. The idea was to free the world from capitalist oppression, imperialist aggression and other such anomalies. Although those expressions sound strange in today's neo-conservative world, they still describe very real sources of evil that are in fact doing as much, if not more, harm nowadays than they were forty years ago. Unfortunately, as I described it in my first book, Mao Zedong and his buddies were at least as oppressive and as aggressive as any of the other ideological zealots of the contemporary period.

This led people like us into promoting exactly the kind of evil that we were supposed to be fighting. At one point, I remember some of us arguing in favor of the Third World War, following Chairman Mao's analysis according to which communism had gained ground mostly because of the First and Second World Wars, and would probably take over what was left of the planet following the next one! Our sectarian zeal had condemned all of us into becoming worse than Nixon and Kissinger, at least on paper.

Like all splinter organizations, we spent most of our time fighting against rival communist groups, rather than genuinely attempting to organize the working-class. The fact that 99% of the blue-collar workers we encountered thought that we were a bunch of idiots made it a lot easier to ignore most of them most of the time. Nevertheless, as apprentice communists, we had to at least try to win some of them over anyway, if only in the long run to have more "real workers" in our tiny group than any other tiny group had. After all, even abstract intellectuals could not spend all of their lives just talking about "concrete action", which was paradoxically the favorite expression of leftists who never did anything real.

For me, one example of this inter-communist rivalry began soon after my little group decided to get jobs in places where real workers spend most of their lives, such as in job-sites organized by trade unions like the Teamsters. In those days, at least in the Toronto area, there was a small caucus from the long-established Communist Party of Canada (CPC) working within that union. They had played what seemed to have been a major role in the excessively violent Ontario Teamsters' strike of 1965. This was of course the same Teamsters' Union that, at least in the USA, had been rightfully accused of being highly indebted to the Mafia for many of its major successes.

Like all the other Maoist affiliates, the PLP and the CPL had already determined that the "Moscow revisionists" of the CPC were a greater danger to the working-class than either the company bosses in Canada or the union leadership in the USA. It so happened that at that time the Teamster bosses from south of the border had already sent a team of investigators, run by an international vice-president, up to Canada to deal with the Communist Party threat. Our "contribution" to the working-class was therefore to tell the union bosses all that we knew (not much, as it turned out) about the CPC caucus within the Toronto local, which obviously helped them, not to mention the Mafia, much more than it helped the workers.

A good punishment for having done this dirty deed, however, was the fact that we then had to put our own lives on the line by standing up at a meeting of Local 938, in front of several hundred extremely angry truck drivers, and trying to explain why we had done what we did. That we were not lynched on the spot is probably due to the fact that the local was about evenly split between those who supported the international leadership and those who had their own reasons for not wanting the CPC caucus to disappear. Needless to say, that ended our own feeble attempts at infiltrating the Teamsters' Union.

Since that time, I have been told about dozens of other similar incidents, regarding Maoist or Trotskyist attempts to "help" other unions with rival communist cells in them, in various Canadian provinces and American states, which apparently had very similar results. My point here is not to pretend that one group of communists were of any more use to the workers than any other group of communists. Nor do I suppose that either union chieftains, Mafiosi, company bosses or government bureaucrats loved the working-class more than the young commies really did. In fact, in spite of all the infighting among the tiny communist groups, or the other wars between the communists and the democratic socialists, or the fights between rival union movements like the Teamsters and the AFL-CIO, workers in North America or any other place were, and are, still better off supporting unions than they are when they let the even more disgusting private entrepreneurs walk all over them.

My point is simply that sectarian extremism leads to a certain kind of abomination, just like investors' greed and government arrogance lead to other kinds of abomination. Because of the way ideas work, every human being who tries to go all the way with any religion or ideology in the real world always ends up doing about the opposite of what he or she originally set out to do! Here are a few more eyewitness examples of what I want to emphasize.

During the same period, I also participated in a number of other fascinating events, with equally disastrous results. At one point, the Toronto CPL set up a front-group known as Canadians for the National Liberation Front, in order to enlarge our involvement in the anti-Vietnam War movement. We went around Canadian cities, as well as joining demonstrations in various American cities, protesting, getting arrested, raising money to get out of jail, and so on. Curiously enough, when we got arrested, the press insisted on calling us "peaceniks", even if our real goal was not peace, but in fact victory for the communist side. Some of this activity may even have had some effect on the eventual American decision to leave Vietnam, although North Vietnamese military efforts probably had a proportionately larger influence!

In any case, at one point we became part of a much larger coalition that had decided to join the April 1967 protests against the Vietnam War taking place simultaneously all over the world. Our group thought that we should prove our militancy by burning an American flag in front of the US consulate in Toronto. However, when a couple of us tried to do just that, we were tackled by a group of policemen and thrown into the paddy wagon, while the rest of the demonstrators were attacked by horses. When the paddy wagon was opened to admit more protestors, we jumped out because someone had yelled that the police were beating up one of our fellow organizers.

Protesting against the war was certainly justified by the fact that most of the two million people who died in that war were killed by US military forces. Trying to burn an American flag was not a crime either, at least not in Canada, which meant that the Toronto police had to justify their actions in court by claiming that the flag fire would have set ablaze the concrete flower boxes that the city had installed in the middle of University Avenue, in front of the consulate! Curiously, the judge at the first trial failed to notice how foolish that argument really was. Later on, however, we managed to convince a more reasonable judge that the whole thing was just too embarrassing.

A few months later, the same coalition then tried to bring the Vietnam War to the 1967 International Exposition (Expo 67) being held in Montreal. After participating in the demonstration against the war in downtown Montreal, miles away from the Expo grounds, a couple of us were sent off to a secret, outdoor meeting with some FLQ members. This was also the period when the Quebec Liberation Front (FLQ) was planting bombs in Canadian mail-boxes, as part of its rather unsympathetic attempt to free Quebec simultaneously from both capitalism and Canadian federalism.

Apparently, the FLQ wanted to extend "fraternal greetings" to our organization, since they had heard that unlike some other tiny communist groups, we also supported Quebec independence. That meeting, however, did not go very well since none of us could really understand any French, while our Quebecois compatriots did not understand that much more English. Several years later, we found out that one of the FLQ members present at that meeting had been assassinated in Paris, on suspicion of being a police informer!

In the end, that little meeting only served to illustrate once again that the "two solitudes", which is to say the historical lack of understanding between English-speaking and French-speaking people in Canada, applied just as much to extremist movements as it did to "bourgeois" outfits. In fact, in spite of a few success stories, socialist and communist organizations of all stripes have seldom been able to understand, much less cooperate with, nationalist movements. Extremists within each ideology most often let their sectarianism overcome any attempts at finding common ground. The same thing could easily be said about inter-faith reconciliation among religious groups, which almost always breaks down over competing doctrines of similar rigidity.

In any case, like all other such organizations, the CPL eventually lost all of its members and became just another historical footnote. My own contribution to extremism, however, also included a stint inside another, even more fascinating group, this one affiliated with Lyndon Larouche. During the early part of the 1970s, a couple of us left the CPL to become the first Canadian members of the just-as-tiny National Caucus of Labor Committees, the name that Larouche was using for his American group at that time.

As I indicated in my first volume, Lyndon Larouche was an ex-Trotskyist organizer in the USA, who started his own sect in order to feed off the New Left movement. Like all the other ultra-communists of that period, he felt that his own brand of the Marxist-Leninist ideology, which was ostensibly based on the writings of a German communist, Rosa Luxemburg, was better than all the others. The one thing that all the other communists (revisionists and ultras) had in common, however, was their undying hatred of comrade Larouche, who they took to be either a CIA or an FBI agent.

Whether or not Larouche was an agent of the CIA or the Vatican is a moot point, but he certainly knew how to make enemies. The Queen of England apparently let him get away with calling her the leader of the international drug-smuggling network, but Henry Kissinger eventually got very upset with being called the most evil person then living. Larouche's anti-communist "mop-up" campaign, which led to a lot of his supporters getting into hundreds of fistfights with every other little communist organization in the Western world, did not help much either.

One of the strangest first-hand experiences I had with this group was during a 1974 conference of Larouche supporters from half a dozen different countries, which was held in New York City. At that time, the Larouche organization was renting out several floors of an old office building in downtown New York equipped with all sorts of files and communications equipment. According to what we were told at the time, a Larouche supporter from Britain had been recently kidnapped in East Germany and brainwashed, then rescued by some of his friends, who promptly set about de-programming him.

This individual apparently informed the startled Larouche organizers that seven Latin frogmen were even then on their way up the East River, bent on assassinating Larouche during that particular conference. Incredible though it may seem, quite a few of the participants were not sure whether or not to believe this "information", and almost everyone was freaking out. Later on, the organization claimed that the paranoia that was so evident at that conference had in fact been encouraged by unnamed outside agents! For me, that was finally enough to get me to end my two-year stint with the NCLC.

A couple of years after I left that group, Larouche turned it away from ultra-communism to a much more ultra-conservative and ultra-nationalist point of view. Apparently, however, the psychological nature of that organization did not change at all, even though, during the Larouchian presidential campaigns of the 1980s, the old left-wing, pro-communist, ideology had been replaced by its theoretical opposite, a right-wing, national-socialist stance. Eventually, Larouche and several of his supporters were jailed for mail fraud and the organization, though it probably still exists, took a real nose-dive.

The seven Latin frogmen, however, were clear evidence that extremism very often leads to considerable mental imbalance. Hundreds of other such examples can easily be gleaned by interviewing people who took part in a whole lot of similar groups.

Unfortunately for me I managed to accumulate still more first-hand experience about this kind of thing several years later on. In my first book, I made several references to the 1975-1979 Khmer Rouge regime in Cambodia, which killed about two million of its own people, in a country with a total population of seven million. This pro-Chinese, ultra-communist government was finally removed by the Vietnamese army, which set up a pro-Vietnamese government lasting until the end of the Cold War. Curiously enough, between 1979 and 1993, countries like Canada and the USA supported the Khmer Rouge government-in-exile, rather than the pro-Soviet communists who were then running Vietnam and Cambodia.

I got marginally involved for a few months in all of this in Montreal, when I decided in 1980 to join a little group of intellectuals that was supporting the Vietnamese side. In Montreal, however, as in dozens of other cities all over the world, a rival group of Khmer Rouge supporters was also established. In fact, the members of both organizations were mostly Southeast Asian students living in Montreal, as well as a few other local supporters of either Soviet or Chinese communism.

On one particular occasion, the China-Khmer Rouge supporters raided a meeting held in Montreal by the USSR-Vietnam supporters, resulting in quite a skirmish. Most of the Canadian citizens on the Khmer Rouge side were members of Maoist organizations like the Workers' Communist Party, which had several dozen followers in Quebec at that time.

The absurdity of the whole thing should have been obvious to everyone involved. In the first place, here we had hundreds of communists fighting among themselves, not only in Asia but also in North America and other places, about which kind of communism was the best, the ultra-totalitarian kind (Maoism) or the less-totalitarian kind (Moscow). More absurd still was the fact that one group of so-called communists was supporting the foreign invasion of another country, while the other group was supporting the mass murder of two million people. In other words, the choice was between a form of imperialism and a form of attempted genocide, two of the main evils that the world communist movement was supposed to be trying to eradicate! Is it any wonder that almost all the tiny Canadian communist parties, whether ultra or revisionist, were dissolved within a year of that particular confrontation?

My own involvement with sectarian stupidity was not yet over, however. During the 1980s, I also decided to support a completely different kind of group, this one working within the nationalist ideology. As I indicated in my first book, nationalism of whatever variety is potentially just as murderous as communism. In fact, since as far back as the fifteenth century, there seems to have been a nationalist element to every mass murder of civilians that took place anywhere in the world. All of the world's leading empires murdered millions of people, for their own nationalist reasons, a fact which has never prevented smaller countries from spawning their own nationalist movements.

One of those movements was the Parti Quebecois, which provided me with a surprisingly similar set of first-hand experiences. As a matter of fact, dozens of English-speaking Canadians, at that time living in Quebec, decided to support the Quebec independence movement for supposedly democratic reasons. We all thought that it was only a matter of time before Quebec became entirely independent from Canada. As it turned out, however, supporting the PQ did not result in any greater degree of political independence or democracy, in Quebec or anywhere else, than supporting Mao Zedong or Lyndon Larouche resulted in any greater freedom or prosperity for the working-class.

One of the major differences between the Parti Quebecois and tiny organizations like the CPL or the NCLC was that the PQ had actually managed to get itself elected. As a result of being in power, if only at the provincial level, it was able to pass laws that were at least supposed to have some sort of real effect in the real world. One such law that was adopted in 1979 and is still in force nowadays, was a reform of the electoral process, which, after many decades of outrageous abuse, had put a complete ban on donations to political parties coming from companies or trade unions. Even individuals could only give a maximum of 3000 $ a year, and all contributions of over 100$ had to be registered in public.

In theory at least, this law made the province of Quebec the most democratic administrative area in North America, since political parties presumably had to represent real citizens instead of corporate, or collective, entities possessing gobs of money. This approach is several light-years away from the American system, in which large private organizations are most often encouraged to control politicians in every possible way.

Like all other democratic reforms, however, the Quebec law has not always been rigidly enforced. Shortly after the law was passed, I myself witnessed one illegal transfer of a reasonably large sum of money at one time, from a rich PQ supporter whose name never showed up on the official register. That supporter was also a senior executive in a company that stood to gain a great deal of business from a PQ government.

It is obvious that that particular law has in fact been violated hundreds of times, by all of the major political parties in Quebec, for very similar reasons. Even though the law is probably still observed more often than not, because it makes such things more difficult to accomplish, corruption never goes away entirely just because some government passes a law against it.

But even the fact that the Parti Quebecois was in power for long periods of time did not prevent its members from splitting up into all sorts of little sectarian entities. During the 1980s, the independence movement was significantly weakened when cock-fighting broke out between the main PQ leaders, about which was the best way to go forward.

The ultras, who desired that Quebec become as independent from Canada as Canada was from the USA (whatever that meant), could not get along with the moderates, who like the general population felt that Quebec should retain some sort of formal economic ties with Canada. Although that difference of opinion was eventually patched up, it helped the federalists win the 1995 referendum on Canadian unity.

As it turned out, the taking of political power by the separatist leaders in Quebec did not ultimately result in the victory of their constitutional option. Nowhere in the world does having political power automatically result in changes taking place that were desired by the rank-and-file supporters of whatever organization came to power. No countries have ever become genuinely communist, or genuinely fascist, or genuinely nationalist, or genuinely democratic, or genuinely Christian or Moslem, simply because one of those ideologies ostensibly took power, by either violent or peaceful means. Governments do not run countries, toxic people do, and no region in the world is run by people who agree with each other sufficiently in order to install any kind of system completely, once and for all. It is not ideology that runs the world, after all, but rather one or more of the various different forms of corruption—such as greed and the desire for power over others.

Sectarian stupidities like the ones that I have witnessed over the past few decades are common to all true believers, whether they belong to extremist political organizations or to psychologically similar religious sects. Unfortunately, this observation also applies to the main organizers and the leading participants in all of the mainstream religious and political organizations. People who have become true believers do not only belong to radical and marginal groups, they also unfortunately belong to much more powerful political institutions.

The unauthorized biographies of all the leading men and women, of whatever culture or period of history, indicate that they were as ideologically diseased as the marginal people we mentioned earlier. Mainstream politicians like Canadian prime ministers or American presidents often turn out to be just as weird, and just as individually harmful, as marginal, paranoid politicians like Lyndon Larouche.

I also managed to personally confirm some of this once again, back in the late 1980s. After I had moved away from the Parti Quebecois organization, I decided to get a close-up look at the newest ideology on the block, neo-conservatism. This was the free-enterprise, anti-government outlook created by such politicians as Margaret Thatcher and Ronald Reagan, which is behind the wave of government cut-backs in social spending that began over twenty years ago and is still going strong nowadays. In fact, it turns out that this "new" conservatism is just the latest version of classical, eighteenth-century liberalism, and is therefore called neo-liberalism in most countries.

For a time, I wrote a number of nonconformist articles for a magazine called "L'Analyste" published in Montreal, whose editorial board supported the Reagan-Thatcher initiative. This group and others like it organized a number of conferences to which they invited hundreds of big-shots from Quebec, from the rest of Canada, and from the USA and Europe, bringing together many CEOs of large corporations, government ministers and leading academics, to discuss the major issues of the day. The idea was to work out ways for bringing about their New World Order of free trade, laissez-faire and fiscal conservatism, which was supposed to do away with big government and make everyone rich in the process.

I got myself invited to several of these conferences as a token nobody and proceeded to discuss the issues with those people. How did they intend to run the world without the Welfare State? How was business going to be able to run everything in a libertarian way, without any government intervention whatsoever? I soon found out that the only participants at those meetings who really believed in complete free enterprise and the total dismantling of all government economic and social programs, were a half dozen fanatic professors. None of the Chief Executive Officers and the Chief Financial Officers present wanted to do away with government altogether; they merely wanted government to go back to the old ways and help them make money, rather than help ordinary people take their money away from them. In other words, they were not upset at Big Government at all; they just wanted the government to help their social class instead of helping all the other social classes!

After that, my last crack at sectarianism took place in 1990-1991, when I was again briefly involved with a very small group of English-speaking Quebeckers who still wanted to support Quebec independence. This was when the provincial governments of the nine Anglophone provinces of Canada had rejected a constitutional compromise worked out by the federal government of that period. Most Quebeckers were very upset at that decision, but the excitement eventually died down, as usual. As it turned out, our tiny little group of Anglophone separatists were simply wasting our time, since the real Quebecois always hedge their bets by never finally deciding, as in 1995, to support either option.

During all those unfortunate years of political involvement, I learned the hard way just how futile it all was. I also found out that the main difference between the marginal examples of political extremism that I have described in this chapter and the mainstream examples that I also mentioned, is simply more power. The leaders of mainstream organizations, such as political parties, governments, and major businesses, are all much more powerful than were any of the extremists that I used to know. There are, of course, vast differences between the power levels of provincial politicians and leaders of major world powers, or the leaders of small businesses and those of multinational corporations, but all of them have more influence on society than do any of the marginal extremists.

Mainstream power, however, means that the sectarianism and the paranoia of "ordinary" politicians and business leaders are much more devastating for the human condition than are any of the marginal examples. It is only when extremists like Mao Zedong succeed in taking power that they are capable of wreaking havoc as great as that as any of the Kissingers and the Bushes.

The words "mainstream" and "extreme" are, after all, merely emanations from political discourse. Lyndon Larouche was more extreme than Henry Kissinger because he did not have political power. Which of the two was the more paranoid is a moot point; which of the two did more harm to humanity is rather obvious. Larouche could have done more harm than Kissinger had he ever succeeded in taking power, but it was Kissinger who came a lot closer to running the world, at least for a few years.

My own quarter-century of political activity only resulted in my getting involved in events which marginally influenced society in mostly harmful ways, the opposite of what I was supposed to be doing. Unfortunately, I found out over the years that communist leaders are not really communist, nationalist leaders are not really nationalist, democratic leaders are not really democratic and libertarian leaders are not really libertarian. Unfortunately for all those who believed in them, either within those organizations or in the general public, all of the people who run organizations, governments and businesses based on any religion or ideology are only really interested in promoting themselves.

IN HARM'S WAY

The fundamental problem underlying most of the social garbage that I have been bitching about in both of my books is that most people are constantly putting each other in harm's way. A lot of the violence which people do to each other is organized, social violence, which often masquerades under such headings as politics, ideology, religion, economics, education, justice and so on. Other violence is more individual, such as I have discussed in the chapters on toxic personalities, discrimination and pets.

As far as I can tell, a lot of people harm each other all the time in order to get ahead of everyone else. This is known in some circles as competition, which requires ambition and aggressiveness in order to function properly. War is one of the main activities for aggressive and ambitious people, the disordered (or toxic) personalities of my first book, while others prefer milder versions of war such as business, sports and administration.

On the other hand, relatively non-aggressive people go through life trying to get along with others, mostly by keeping out of their way as much as humanly possible. This kind of people are at their happiest when they are alone, or with only one or two other people who are a lot like them. When they go to work, they actually try to do the jobs that they have been assigned to accomplish, to the best of their abilities. They want to be properly remunerated for those efforts, but they do not spend all of their time trying to figure out ways to get more out of the system than they have put into it.

Ambitious and aggressive people, the world's psychologically challenged, or toxic personalities, are not at all like the meek. Instead, toxic people like to hang out with the largest number of other people as possible, so that they can prove their prowess with a larger audience and thereby become the life of the party. When they go to work, they spend most of their time trying to dominate others, so as to get everyone else to do all the work. They are constantly trying to figure out new ways to get the system to work for them.

If they have to work for a living, aggressive people always try to do the least amount of work possible, for the largest possible reward. If they are someone else's customers, they do their damnedest to pay the least amount of money possible, in exchange for the most service possible. If they are someone else's merchants, they try to avoid giving any service whatsoever, while trying to get paid much more than for what they are worth.

Aggressive people love to attack others, because this gives them a sense of domination, which in their minds means the same as achievement. They are constantly playing a zero-sum game, in which the only way to get ahead is to take something away from someone else. This is another reason why, as I discussed earlier, property is theft, simply because those who pursue the property principle think in the same way that thieves think.

This is why the worst thing that a meek employee can say to an aggressive boss is that he or she has given ten, twenty, thirty, forty or fifty years of loyal service to the employer, and that he or she therefore deserves to be treated better. Toxic personalities immediately react to this kind of complaint by baring their fangs. For them, loyal service can only be given by a weak person, someone who does not realize that life supposedly means giving nothing to anyone, least of all loyalty. People in charge "know" that life is about getting as much as possible out of everybody else. They are enraged at the meek person's attitude, especially since loyal service shows up their own shortcomings as egotistical maniacs.

Instead, aggression means winning, either by killing more of the enemy's population than they are capable of killing one's own population, or by scoring more goals than the opposing team, or by accumulating more capital than the other investor, or by getting away with more crimes than all the other criminals. Winning is everything to aggressive people and it justifies any kind of rotten activity, just so long as that rottenness does not blow up in the aggressor's face. He or she will kill, maim, rape, steal, destroy, deceive, lie or cheat—just so long as none of those things gets in the way of success. Niccolo Machiavelli did not invent anything; he merely described the kind of reality that we now call Machiavellian.

In fact, the key word here is rape. Essentially, what the aggressor wants is to cause violence to his or her adversary. Violence is not an unfortunate consequence of trying to get ahead, violence is not just used (as in war) because the other side started it; it is the number one goal of the aggressive individual. Harming the other person is what ambition is all about, since it is the only way to prove the aggressor's superiority over others.

This is why the French word for rape is "viol", which is the root of violence. "Viol" means getting the best of someone else, triumphing over the adversary, degrading and belittling another human being. Force, brutality and outrage are what ambitious and aggressive people want the most, so that the other person should be hurt and harmed as much as is humanly possible.

In this imagined zero-sum world, degrading and downgrading everyone else is the only way to glorify and to upgrade the aggressor's status. This is why all those people who run things, such as countries or armies, or companies, or hospitals or schools or whatever, run them first and foremost to prove to everyone under them just how "worthy" the bosses really are. Social status is the name of the game, and has to be proven and driven home over and over again by having the boss do something horrible to someone else, anyone else, just in order to inspire eternal fear and respect among all the underlings.

Doing violence unto others is the lifetime goal of "winners", those who feel that they were born to dominate. The violence is never gratuitous, but always essential to preserve the dominator's sense of well-being. The rape involved is what makes it fun for the person on top. It makes no difference whatsoever if the rape is heterosexual or homosexual, as long as it clearly demonstrates who the boss is.

The quintessential form of rape is its original form, which is to say the sexual penetration of someone else's body without the other person's permission. In this most primitive form of rape, the rapist or the violator feels that if "God" had not wanted men to rape women, "He" would not have put an appendage on one sex and a receptor on the other. According to the twisted logic of the rapist, women who refuse sex are therefore acting against natural law, since the aggressor would not feel like dominating if he had not been made to dominate. This is why Moslem fanatics require their women to cover their entire bodies and faces, because those fanatical men are so primitive that they naturally assume that any real man will always and forever try to rape any uncovered woman he happens to see in public.

The truth of the matter, however, is that 90% of all victims in all parts of the world are raped at home by members of their own family. Given this fact, the tribal rule about covering women from head to toe seems to be just a way of keeping all the victims within the family and not allowing even 10% of the potential victims to get away from family control! Keeping it all in the family is undoubtedly a very cohesive social strategy.

Even in those cases in which the victim did not know the rapists, however, many people still go out of their way to blame the victim for whatever happens to her. For example, this is what happened to the white woman back in 1989 who was jogging after 9 P. M. in New York's Central Park. After having been raped, beaten and left for dead by one or several young hooligans, apparently of Latin American origin, she also had to put up with the fact that, even years afterward, Puritanical Americans still blame her for the whole situation, since she should never have gone into a public park after dark! It seems that the natural law of Puritanism obliges all young men to behave like wild dogs and also justifies sloppy police work and lenient attitudes toward potential murderers.

A much more recent (2003), if more comical, event involved a Canadian woman who was harassed while breast-feeding her baby on an airline flight within the USA. Apparently, one American on the same flight felt oppressed by this foreign national and wanted the woman thrown off the plane for obnoxious behavior. After all, from a Puritanical point of view, that Canadian breast was terrorizing good American citizens in the same way that foreign dictators all over the world get the born-again US President so upset by daring to be different. The herd instincts of the physically superior person are outraged whenever some "inferior" person insists on doing things that "Our Gang" finds intolerable.

How could anyone dare to be so un-American as to bare her breast in public? Even if some American women probably do the same thing from time to time, apparently it is still intolerable for an alien to perform the same act in American airspace. Even though such Puritanical or neo-conservative points of view are as collectively and as socially based as any other points of view always are, contradictions of this sort should never prevent good, old-fashioned, free citizens from trying to defend their own individual rights!

Think about all the different ways in which breastfeeding is un-American. In the first place, it is an obvious refusal to allow the universal sale of milk substitutes, which undermines the free-enterprise economy. Depriving companies of sales is also contrary to the North American Free Trade Agreement, which clearly stipulates that all products and services must be merchandisable. Breastfeeding also undermines the century-old American effort to fashion the female breast into an exclusive sex object, not to be used for any more mundane purposes. It therefore potentially deprives advertising agencies of much of their impact on consumers, as well as depriving all red-blooded American males of their inherent right to be sexually titillated whenever the female breast appears in public. Last but not least, breastfeeding may also be a communist act since it also denies the individual liberties of those private citizens who prefer to separate sex and reproduction!

The same kind of twisted logic is also used in more serious cases, such as whenever politically-correct intellectuals claim that African societies are perfectly justified in excising young women's clitorises in order to keep them faithful to their husbands, or that Moslem cultures are justified in preserving polygamy. In reality, however, aggression against the weaker members of society cannot be upheld for cultural reasons any more than it can be upheld on the grounds of natural law. The same sort of fascist thinking is also evident when certain anthropologists and documentary film-makers uphold the right of Neolithic tribes to continue practicing circumcision in open-air ceremonies. Non-medical circumcision of babies is a hideous practice anyway, no matter in what circumstances it takes place nor for what religious purposes.

In the same vein, from the aggressor's point of view, male rape victims become just unreal, weak men whose incapacity to physically resist rape is proof of their similarity to women. Finally, rapists also believe that the strongest person on Earth is the best person on Earth, since that is the way that God, or Mother Nature, made the world. This, by the way, is also the main reason why most Christians and Moslems believe that God is good, simply because he is so incredibly powerful: might makes right!

All other forms of rape are derivatives from the original form. Investors who succeed, who have made it, are considered to have triumphed over their inferiors—those who made less money, or those whose work has been successfully exploited for the benefit of others, or those customers who got fewer services than for what they actually paid.

By the same logic, administrators who succeed therefore must be those who force other people to work for them, for less money than what the workers deserve, while making them submit to more compulsory overtime. Generals who succeed also become those who convince millions of soldiers to die for them, while simultaneously killing millions of enemies, soldiers and civilians, not to mention raping as many enemy women as humanly possible. According to "winners", success means urinating in the mouths of everyone else.

Therefore, according to this domination or superman philosophy (Friedrich Nietzsche), good does not exist without evil: good is what makes an aggressor feel superior, while evil is the fate of inferiors. Harm is required for others, so that relief may come to the dominant. The best kinds of relief are the really complicated ones, which really prove a dominator's prowess, beyond the shadow of a doubt.

For example, what could be better than bravery in war? A general of some country succeeds in convincing some soldier to sacrifice his own life in some particularly courageous way, against overwhelming odds, to save his fellow soldiers from enemy fire. Everyone is ecstatic about what an amazing fellow the dead ignoramus really was, how selfless his act. All that he did, however, was to commit suicide so that the general's side could kill more enemy soldiers than his own side lost. This is just the highest kind of bravery for the lowest kind of activity. How really proud the general must feel to have successfully raped that brave soldier's mind: the simpleton died so that the general could kill even more simpletons. Glory, glory, hallelujah!

This is what ambition and aggression are really all about. Rape someone else, anyone else, in a mild way (through sloppy work, price-gouging, or giving someone an unjustified dressing-down), in a medium way (fire a rebellious employee, slap a spouse in the face, or win an election) or in a really violent way (commit war, sexual rape, or, best of all, genocide). Demonstrate superiority, macho masculinity, racism, social domination, business acumen, sportsmanship and be in the winners' circle: that is what life is all about for the people on top.

The best possible confirmation of my basic argument can be found in the September 2001, Islamic war on New York and Washington, as well as the American counterattack. What a way to underline exactly what I am saying about the world's leading aggressors! People like bin Laden are only nominal Islamists, who use the Moslem religion for their own personal purposes. What is important for such people is their ability to use a radical interpretation of belief in order to get other people to commit suicide for their real masters. Whatever Allah or Mohamed, or some later caliph, may have actually written in the Koran, whatever the majority of the world's Moslem clerics or followers may really think about terrorism, is of no consequence to such people. Instead, bin Laden and Company thoroughly enjoyed the incredible rush of being able to wipe out 3000 people in just a few minutes, especially if most of them were not Moslems and Arabs, but were instead Christians and Jews, Americans and Europeans.

The people who actually carry out such suicide attacks most probably believe in Allah and the Moslem version of heaven, but their leaders most probably only believe in themselves. After all, Moslem extremists like bin Laden are constantly speculating on the world's financial markets, making money with money, regardless of the fact that usury seems to have been specifically condemned by their religion. True believers like the Taliban received much of their revenue from the heroin trade, and all other kinds of illicit activities, even though those illegal activities are also specifically condemned in their belief system. In fact, such people do not really care about religious purity; they simply go about finding some theological justification or another, so that they can continue doing whatever they please. The important thing is to get others to do their bidding, to get the kind of high that can only be achieved by raping someone else's mind or body. Dictators like Saddam Hussein may not have the same ideology as the bin Laden crowd, but they do share the same general attitude toward ordinary people.

The same thing can also be said about George Bush, Junior, or any of his predecessors. Any person who becomes the president of the world's most powerful nation is not really up there in order to preserve democracy, or freedom, or any of the other code words currently being used. Like bin Laden, Bush desperately needs the kind of rush that comes from ordering a worldwide crackdown on something or other, and causing the deaths of several thousand more people. As a true believer in "America" (the USA), Bush is not the least bit worried that his actions will inevitably reduce the already inadequate levels of democracy and freedom that most North Americans were enjoying prior to the September 11, 2001 attack. Killing civilians in the Middle East, sending American soldiers to their often self-inflicted doom: these are the things that give a powerful person a natural high.

This does not mean that bin Laden, Hussein and Bush are exactly the same kind of person. Liberal capitalism and democracy are much better ideologies than are fascism and Islamic fundamentalism, at the very least because books such as this one could never be published in any country or region run by people like Ossama bin Laden or Saddam Hussein. People like Bush, however, do not choose freedom and democracy as operating slogans, as opposed to such other slogans as sharia and jihad, because they really intend to be genuine democrats. As I noted in my first book, leaders of so-called free nations adopt their liberal slogans because this is what is expected of them, and because they have discovered that far more people will do their bidding if they use those slogans than if they use any other ones.

Once again, as the British philosopher, Bertrand Russell pointed out during the Cold War, "In a democracy we have our freedoms until we need them." Following a major terrorist attack, what better moment to enjoy the freedoms that are supposed to be guaranteed by democratic government? But even though the September 11 attack, or any of the other more recent attacks, was not big enough to erase individual liberty completely, there is no doubt that fewer of those freedoms now exist than were in place only a few short years ago. If bin Laden's group is capable of launching another really big attack within the next few years, or if some other equally calamitous events take place, such as a botched invasion of North Korea, then democratic freedoms will be curtailed even more.

At some point, rights and freedoms may even disappear altogether, just like they did during the Great Depression and the Second World War. Even during the relatively easy war to get rid of Saddam Hussein, the right to dissent was also under attack, particularly in the USA, as the fellow in upstate New York found out when he was arrested for disturbing the peace (!) by wearing a pacifist T-shirt in a shopping center.

What is important for the powerful person is the need to get his or her daily fix by influencing other people's lives in any number of ways. Killing other people is the biggest high, but ordering them around is almost as good. This observation applies just as much to business leaders as it does to political leaders, and just as much to any other kind of big shot (university rectors, orchestra leaders, popes, you name it). Wielding power, whether it comes in the form of a presidential order, a large stock-exchange deal, a papal bull or an Islamic fatwa, is what the world's most important rapists are mainly interested in achieving.

Censorship of news also makes such people feel more powerful, whether they are terrorist leaders or presidents. Even minor inconveniences for other people, such as longer lineups at airports or border crossings, help salvage such empty, unloving souls from their inner sense of worthlessness. The bin Ladens, the Husseins, the Bushes, the Chiracs and the Putins are the ones who need these fixes the most often, but the same psychological confirmation is also sought by every other human being, at whatever level of power, who chooses to lord it over others.

Another interesting case in point is the large-scale theft and vandalism that occurred after the Saddam Hussein regime fell in Iraq. This "untidy" event was officially treated by the Bush administration as an unfortunate consequence of the Iraqi people having been cooped up so long by a major dictator. In fact, it was just another planned consequence of the invasion itself, since most of the world's buyers of stolen goods are to be found in the richest countries. The actual planning may have been an inside job or the work of international crime syndicates, but the people who run such syndicates are often the same people as those who run major governments. The vandalism in Iraq or in any other war was not all that much different from the vandalism involved in any of the world's major financial scandals.

This untidy attitude may also help to explain why gun control is not on the Bush government's agenda, any more than it is on the Moslem terrorists' agenda. Theoretically, since the USA is so much more interested in "homeland security" nowadays than it was in the past, everything should be done to bring that about. Curiously, however, among all the different measures having been adopted to increase security, Attorney-General John Ashcroft has most definitely not included gun control. Instead, he has interpreted one of the amendments to the US Constitution, the one about the right of ordinary citizens to bear arms, in the most literal fashion possible. No one will ever be able to explain to a born-again Christian that increasing the number of guns in free circulation will never contribute anything to homeland security. Trying to do so would be like trying to explain to a pot-head that increased marijuana consumption is not a fundamental human right.

Getting lots of money, for very little effort, is what motivates many other egomaniacs. Currency speculators, drug dealers, stock manipulators, people smugglers, the list is endless. It also includes the directors of agencies like the FBI and the CIA, who received billions of dollars from their government without ever providing their country with the kind of protection that they were being paid to provide. This is the same type of intelligence failure which occurs when the Hell's Angels biker gang fails to provide adequate protection to "its" local merchants from raids being carried out by rival gangs, such as the Bandidos. All kinds of incompetent people are always getting paid billions, in exchange for very little useful service. What a rush that can be!

The leaders of all these different human organizations, such as the government of the USA, or the United Nations, or the Al-Qaeda terrorist network, or the Hell's Angels biker gang, are always telling everyone that they have to choose sides. Bush Junior repeated the classic admonition after the September 11 terrorist attack: You are either with us or you are against us. In fact, every single organization which has ever existed, from the first Sumerian city-state right up to the present day, has always come up with one version or another of the same message: It is always us or them.

Unfortunately for all of the world's leaders, this statement is always a lie. If we take the Bush statement as a typical example, the unreality of the American president's point of view becomes immediately obvious.

The point is that in the fight against terrorism, the USA itself has never been entirely on one side or on the other. This is not just because of the rather remote possibility that the Bush administration may have set up the whole September 11 scenario by itself, or at least deliberately failed to stop the Moslem extremists from carrying out their nefarious deeds. Nor is it only because of the rather obvious involvement of the Saudi rulers in the terrorist attacks, or of the Bush cabinet's well-known business relations with those same Saudis.

Instead, throughout the American Revolution, as well as in every single year of its existence since that time, the USA has been as actively involved in promoting terrorism, somewhere in the world, as it has been in eradicating it. Whenever the geopolitical situation warranted it, the USA has itself used terror, or supported the use of the terror weapon by any one of its temporary allies. Most of the members of the current Afghan government are only one of the most recent examples of terrorists who have received extensive support from the American government.

As has been already pointed out by thousands of other observers all over the world, the USA is not currently interested in attacking any terrorist organizations except the ones that it chooses to attack. Most of the other terrorist groups on the planet may continue going about their daily business without any opposition coming from the world's only superpower. The fact that Ossama bin Laden and his entire network were originally US allies and assets against the USSR is simply one more way of proving that the current war on terrorism is not really directed against terrorism as such. Needless to say, Saddam Hussein was also a US ally at one point, as a matter of fact precisely when he was mistreating his own population the most.

The same kind of observation applies to every other "us or them" situation that every other country, or every other human organization of any sort, has ever tried to create. In the religious wars of the sixteenth and seventeenth centuries, for example, Christian rulers often sided with Moslem rulers against other Christians, and Catholic countries often sided with Protestant countries against other Catholic countries. All sides were always part of the other sides! The same sort of thing took place again during the Second World War, when the Western democracies first teamed up with the fascist powers against Soviet totalitarianism (Munich,

1938), then watched the two totalitarian ideologies team up against them (the Hitler-Stalin Pact, 1939-1941), then supported one totalitarian ideology against the other (1941-1945).

Similar mix-ups occur all the time even in non-military conflicts. Countries ostensibly lobbying for free trade often include different forms of protectionism in their package deals with other countries. In a more or less similar fashion, the person who spends the most time consoling the families of murder victims often turns out to be the murderer himself! Opposing sides almost always end up being part of the same sides.

Another excellent example is the war on drugs, which several countries have also been officially waging for the past several decades, using the same sort of international coalition currently being used in the war on terrorism. The USA in particular has spent hundreds of billions of dollars ostensibly trying to eradicate the heroin trade in Afghanistan and in Southeast Asia, or the cocaine trade in South America. At the same time, the population of the USA is the world's largest consumer of both products! Corrupt officials in the USA and everywhere else have been helping criminal organizations, both foreign and American, market these products all over the world, but especially within the USA, for the simple reason that that country happens to have the largest concentration of available wealth in the world. In Afghanistan, for example, two or three years into the American military occupation, the production of heroin has enormously increased rather than declined as it theoretically should have.

Countries get involved in the war on drugs in the same way that they get involved in the war on terrorism. They are also involved in various other "wars" in exactly the same manner. Another well-known example is any member country's participation in the Organization of Economic Cooperation and Development's attempt to rid the world of tax havens like Liechtenstein and the Cayman Islands. In fact, there are certainly a thousand times more citizens of those countries involved in promoting those tax havens than there are citizens working against them. The same observation definitely applies to every member country within the OECD, such as Canada, whose leaders often own major corporations operating out of the world's best-known tax havens. In fact, the USA is only more corrupt than other leading nations because it is economically bigger than any of the other countries.

To put it plainly, none of the world's countries actually belong to the people who live in them, nor do any of the other organizations of any sort on this planet actually belong to their members. Various groups and factions among the world's leaders are always using every government and every other organization to carry out all sorts of unofficial goals, most of which are not at all in the best interests of most of the world's people.

Like every other country, the USA is in fact under the control of geopolitical morons and financial hobgoblins who constantly use that country's military and economic power for their own factional purposes. Their nefarious projects have to be adapted to the prevailing political, economic, social and cultural characteristics of the American people, but these projects do not belong to the American population as a whole. Since the world began, every other country, and every other human institution, has always behaved in the same fashion. Iraq is not the only country in the world whose leadership has often acted like a Mafia family.

Another fascinating example of the same syndrome is the reaction to Norman Finkelstein's book about the holocaust industry. In that book, Finkelstein demonstrated that the Zionist movement has itself belittled the Nazi holocaust against the Jews by deflecting most of the compensation payments made by Germany and various other countries away from the victims and their families, and into its own coffers. Since the book came out, however, anti-Semites have been using it for their own purposes, while Zionists have been accusing Finkelstein and anyone who agrees with his argument as being anti-Semites!

This is just another version of the same "us or them" schoolyard game that George Bush, Ariel Sharon, Saddam Hussein, Ossama bin Laden and the Saudi royal family have also been playing. As I emphasized already in my first book, a pox on all your houses! Skeptics like me do not have to choose between the Zionists and the anti-Semites any more than we have to choose between the American Empire and its terrorist adversaries. The Israeli example is particularly edifying since it is obvious that anti-Semitism is Zionism's biggest ally: how else can most Jews be persuaded that they cannot live with Gentiles except through anti-Semitism? In this as in every other case, the opposing sides in fact help each other control their own subject populations. We can reject all of these prejudiced outlooks as long as we stick with the facts to the best of our abilities, trying to uncover every evil deed committed by every group, without ever exaggerating, or underestimating, the number of people who have been harmed or murdered by every organized group of marauders in human history.

The Jewish people killed by the Nazis during the Holocaust do not belong to the Zionist leaders any more than the Nazi movement actually belonged to the German people. Ordinary people are quite capable of participating in mass murder, in Germany or anywhere else, but ordinary people never actually control any of the institutions that regularly commit mass murder. That role always belongs to the toxic personalities who run every organization. As Finkelstein has shown, ordinary people do not run the Zionist movement either. Nor do they run Israel, the PLO, Al-Qaeda, Saudi Arabia or the government of the USA. Not to mention Syria or North Korea!

Precisely the same kind of thinking is required when dealing with such events as the 2001 United Nations conference on racism, held that year in South Africa. Aside from the Israeli-Arab conflict, the other major debate at that conference was about possible compensation for the slave trade of the seventeenth, eighteenth and nineteenth centuries. Once again, if some sort of compensation is eventually paid, it will inevitably end up in the wrong hands. Black Africa, or even Haiti, certainly suffered from that trade to a tremendous extent, to the same extent in fact as the Arab, the European and the American traders benefited from it. But the people who will end up spending any potential reward monies will undoubtedly be people like Liberia's Charles Taylor, the ideological descendants of the same African kings who sold their prisoners of war to the slave traders in the first place!

So there it is. People with no power, or very little power, are always and forever being placed in harm's way by people with more power, especially by those who wield a great deal of power. Hundreds of thousands of egomaniacs are out there every day, eagerly raping billions of relatively innocent victims. Evil for the many is good for the few.

The people who create most of the harm are the people in power, the toxic personalities of this world. They came to power, and they remain in power, specifically because they are evil people, and not in spite of that.

Their goal is to hurt others and no amount of righteous argument will ever have any positive effect on them.

This is because powerful persons are necessarily two-dimensional thinkers. They are so incredibly blinded by their naked ambition and individual egoism that they are totally incapable of any kind of three or four-dimensional thought, on any kind of deeper, non-superficial level. People like Saddam Hussein, Ossama bin Laden, several Saudi princes and George Bush the Second, who all apparently spent their youth boozing and womanizing in nightclubs, have many things in common, of which the most important is their incapacity to recognize anything which does not serve their own individual interests.

As two-dimensional thinkers, they can vaguely perceive the existence of some sort of shadowy "other world", but they are obliged by their ideological blinkers to dismiss other points of view by using different kinds of ideological slogans. Attackers are either infidels or madmen, while skeptics are dismissed as if they were sorcerers or aliens. The two-dimensional mind is incapable of perceiving anything beyond its own mental prison, which prevents the powerful from ever being able to escape any of the knee-jerk reactions that they are so fond of performing.

As for ordinary people, all they can do about any of these events is to make impotent conversation. After the 2001 terrorist attack on the USA, people all over the world, but especially in North America, suddenly began talking about what had to be done, just like the Australians did after the 2002 Bali attack. As in the Great Depression or the Second World War, conversation instantly shifted to apportioning the blame and deciding how to respond. In the American case, many leading citizens argued for a major military strike against Afghanistan, while others made as if the war had not already begun and advocated peace instead.

For a skeptic to participate in such conversations is particularly difficult. On the one hand, it is obvious that the retaliatory killing of vast numbers of innocent civilians, as has happened so often in the past, only increases the number of people in poor countries who have good reason to detest Western imperialism. On the other hand, it is just as obvious that the Islamic terrorists have already been at war with the West for several centuries, and that being nice to them will not necessarily reduce the number of victims that they plan to go on killing over the next few decades. Also inadequate is pointing out how many of the Islamic terrorists were in fact courted, trained and financed by American agencies as geopolitical allies against the USSR and Iran.

A lot of the debate still centers on whether or not the USA, or any other victimized nation, actually deserved to receive a terrorist attack. In that sense, the September 11 event was typical of all the others. The answer is that while the USA certainly deserved it, most of the people in the World Trade Center and the Pentagon did not. In this case as well as in so many other such cases, most observers routinely make the mistake of confounding a country's leadership with its people. With totalitarian countries, the distinction between the government and the general population is always easier to make than it is with officially democratic countries. However, in every case, no government ever really represents the majority of its people.

The leaders of the USA, both in politics and in business, most certainly did deserve to be attacked. There is no doubt about the fact that they have killed millions of people over the years, most of them recently. Their victims included Black slaves and Black protesters within the USA, American Indians and Mexicans, Civil War cannon fodder, strikers and protesters of all origins from 1783 to the present, civilian victims and cannon fodder during the world wars and colonial peoples from all over the world, in such places as the Philippines, Korea, Vietnam, Indonesia, the Congo, Angola, Cuba, Nicaragua and Iraq. In many of those cases, the leaders of the USA have received help in the killing of all those people, from various other big shots, of all sorts of different origins. Nevertheless, the bosses of the world's largest empire, at least since the Americans replaced the British by controlling the largest empire, were undoubtedly more responsible for those deaths than any of the other leaders were.

Unfortunately, most of the people who died in the 2001 attack, and all the other terrorist attacks in the world, were not big shots. Most of them were just ordinary people going about their daily affairs. Very few of the victims of terrorism have ever been the kind of leading politicians and CEOs whose daily decisions in fact resulted in the deaths of millions of other ordinary people. When the terrorists attack and the imperialists counter-attack, very few big chiefs end up dead.

The same sort of thing takes place in wars, revolutions, rebellions, riots, strikes, protests and all sorts of other violent events. "Indirect violence" such as most of the major famines, depressions and civil wars should also be included, since each of these murderous events often includes a significant element of deliberate decision making. The decisions to kill large numbers of ordinary people, whether directly or indirectly are always taken by some kind of chieftain, either a politician, an army general, a company president, a leader of a populist movement or a leader of a terrorist organization.

Of course, many of the ordinary people behind such leaders do quite often approve of many of these murderous decisions. Millions of ordinary citizens actively participate in direct violence, either as soldiers or as rioters. Millions of other ordinary citizens also benefit from indirect violence, such as from the Western control of petroleum products that was one of the objectives of the Gulf War in 1990-1991 and of the 2003 war against Iraq.

Nevertheless, this does not exonerate any of the leaders from any of the murderous decisions made, ostensibly on behalf of the nations or the social groups that they are supposed to represent. No human institution is now, ever has been or ever will be run as a genuine democracy. It is in fact thoroughly impossible to consult the entire population of any human grouping, by direct referendum, every time that any decision has to be made.

No leader is capable, much less willing, of organizing daily, clearly worded, plebiscites on every subject, while simultaneously providing the entire population with all the information necessary to make an entirely informed decision about everything. If such a thing were possible, the results might still be similar to what the leaders have actually brought about anyway. But the chances are good that millions of ordinary human beings would hesitate quite often to condemn millions of other ordinary human beings to certain death. This type of speculation is beside the point, however, since decision-making will certainly never take place in this way.

A much more useful contribution to this debate is to point out that bin Laden's gang, as well as George Bush's gang or Jacques Chirac's gang, do not give a goddamn what individual people with no power may be saying about all this. As in all such previous situations, since human history began, the people in power always do whatever they were going to do anyway, regardless of what powerless individuals may think. It makes no difference whatever to the big shots what the people down at the water-cooler may say, or may not say, at least individually.

Whenever the terrorists strike, as they inevitably continue to do, they will attack any and all Westerners who happen to be within range of their weapons. It will not make any difference to them whether or not such and such a group of people favor all-out Western retaliation against the terrorist enemy, while such and such another group prefer unilateral peace ("turn the other cheek"). As has happened every single time in the past, when mass murder takes place the pacifists end up just as dead as the warmongers. No amount of economic aid or social reconciliation will make the terrorists' hatred of Westerners disappear, since that hatred is mostly based on ideological fanaticism, not just on poor job prospects.

Similarly, during the period when the Empire strikes back, as all of them inevitably do, they must also attack all those human beings who are within range of their weapons. American, British, French, Russian, Indian and Chinese soldiers, intelligence agents and border-crossing guards will not always distinguish between enemies and neutrals. Innocent people will continue to die in large numbers, either because they happen to belong to the same ethnic or religious groups as the dictators or the terrorists, or because they happen to be in the wrong place at the wrong time. In spite of all their highly touted democratic values, neither the UK nor the USA, not to mention any of the less democratic countries, will have the opportunity or the desire to spare the peacemongers.

In totalitarian or theocratic countries, such as Afghanistan still is, people are regularly put in jail merely for expressing a contradictory opinion. In democratic countries such as the USA or France, this does not happen nearly as often. Dissenters and neutrals can usually express their anti-imperialism without always ending up in prison, though most of them are usually silenced anyway by their fear of the imperial patriots who live beside them. In Canada and in some parts of Western Europe, the situation is somewhat better than it is in the USA, since anti-imperialism amounts to radical chic in those countries, and is even popular among certain intellectuals.

But whatever the situation, the points of view of powerless

individuals count for nothing, and are never considered, no matter what they advocate. This is why conversations taking place in democratic countries are so worthless. It is part of the definition of democracy, such as it is, for leaders to simply ignore other people's individual opinions. Let me be very clear about this: leaders do not easily ignore the organized opinions of millions of people, but they do ignore the individual opinions of millions of unorganized dissenters. In any event, large numbers of people rarely oppose their government in any concerted fashion.

In every political situation, whether democratic or totalitarian, leaders cannot afford to completely ignore the mass movements that do occasionally spring up. Most of the time, however, they can count on basic human reactions to engender the kinds of mass emotions that can be readily manipulated by them. With the proper amount of manipulation, leaders can usually succeed in directing mass movements in whatever direction they deem appropriate.

Large groups of people never express the kind of universal skepticism that I am advocating in my books. They can normally be relied upon to support the kind of ideological slogan mongering which the leaders of the world are so efficient at providing. Bin Laden uses slogans such as Islam, the Koran, sharia, fatwa and jihad, while Bush uses slogans like democracy, the Bible, the rule of law and human rights. Those tremendously efficient slogans are then used to justify either terrorist attacks or imperialist retribution, which only lead to more terrorist attacks and more imperialist retribution later on.

This is why all the endless commentary that continues to fill the world media, about what the USA, or the terrorist organizations, or the United Nations, or anybody else, should or should not do about some current situation, is so incredibly worthless. What human institution has ever done something, or refrained from doing something, because of what some journalist said on the evening news, or wrote in the morning paper? No government, or terrorist group, or spy organization, or political party, or religious denomination, is going to change its policy based on the normative pleadings of some editorialist!

Terrorism is not going to end any time soon, nor is retaliation against terrorism. Some particular group of terrorists may be successfully eliminated at some particular time in some particular country, for whatever reason, but terrorism itself is never going to disappear. Evil of that nature will live on forever, along with war, and famine, and all the different kinds of inequality. The Bushes and the Blairs, the Chiracs, the bin Ladens and the Charles Taylors of this world need all those different forms of evil, so that they can go on proving to everyone else just how important really ambitious people obviously are.

Cock-fighting between rival ambitions was also one of the main features of the 2003 see-saw over whether or not "the world" should invade Iraq. The USA, Britain, France, Germany, Russia and China all claim to have suspected that Iraq may still have had various kinds of weapons of mass destruction in its arsenal, even during the economic boycott of the 1990s. Regardless of what the UN inspectors might have found, those countries thought that way presumably because they were the powers who sold those weapons to Iraq in the first place. When the Anglo-American coalition forces eventually arrived in Iraq, they also claimed to have been astounded to discover that the Iraqis had really destroyed most of the weapons that they had originally worked so hard to stockpile. Then they wondered how could anyone have been so stupid as to actually destroy such useful items, or to have hidden them so well as to render them useless.

In fact, the only really astounding stupidity is that months after the end of the war, the US Army was still officially looking for non-existent weapons and millions of people were still officially expecting them to be found. Obviously, if such weapons had really existed they would immediately have been used to preserve the Hussein regime from total disintegration. In any case, the diplomatic battle over war on Iraq was not really about weapons, since dozens of other irresponsible politicians (especially George Bush) possess many more weapons than Iraq ever did.

That battle was certainly about the control of petroleum reserves and about the geopolitical control of Iraq as a potential pivot for total control over the entire Middle East. Obviously, no one in power could care less about what a tautology it was to pretend to be intolerant of totalitarianism, because totalitarianism is so intolerant!

However, the psychological aspect was just as important. Leading politicians like to dominate other people; it is in fact their number one goal in life. No one who runs the world's only superpower wants anyone else pushing him around, while the leaders of lesser powers like France, Germany, Russia, China and even Iraq like nothing better than to assert whatever level of independence they can muster. Leaders of minor countries in Eastern Europe, Africa and Latin America also enjoyed being courted by all the major powers for similar reasons. The whole thing was an enormous cock-fight, with all the hens (the powerless people of the world) standing around clucking impotently.

Nor should straightforward racism be left out of the account. Several American columnists did everyone a favor during the months following the war when they pointed out that one good reason for having the coalition attack Iraq was that it was an Arab country. According to these people, some Arab country, any Arab country had to be hit and not just non-Arab Afghanistan, because the 9/11 terrorists were all Arabs and the USA had to get its revenge on Arabs, not just on Moslems. It was even argued that taking on the most vulnerable of all the Arab countries was supposedly a good idea since all terrorism is tacitly supported by governments and that was the best way to scare all the Arab governments into being more cowardly in the future!

To be sure, the USA and Britain were also upset at Hussein for signing deals with every customer except them, so they invaded Iraq in order to put a more cooperative comprador in place. But then they had the even greater gall to turn around and call that operation "compassionate imperialism", arguing in the British newspapers that the "moral superiority" of the Anglo-American coalition was similar to the British Navy's nineteenth-century attempt to abolish the slave trade! Aside from the fact that the slave trade was never really abolished, that comparison was particularly disgusting because of the millions of native peasants that the British Army simultaneously herded into forced-labor camps in British plantations all over the world.

This most recent version of compassionate imperialism also apparently included the almost one million Iraqis killed since 1990, mostly by the United Nations embargo. The 2003 invasion of Iraq, like the 2001 invasion of Afghanistan, was also prompted by the same kind of accusations against the local dictator which Britain used so often a hundred years ago: the bad guy has been stockpiling weapons, he has been mistreating local tribes and/or missionaries and/or foreign merchants, and he is not civilized like Westerners are. It also had the same kind of war strategy: first, disarm the bad guy for several years before attacking, and then divide the invaded country into ethnic zones, getting some tribes and religious groups to support the invasion and neutralizing others. Finally, it had the same results: put in a new government composed of pro-imperialist "nigger kings", local politicians who will cooperate with the invaders. All along, it also helps to pretend that the bad guy was a real threat to imperial armies possessing a hundred thousand times more fire-power.

In reality, all of the nonconformist regimes which have been attacked by the USA and its allies since the end of the Cold War (Panama in 1989, Iraq in 1991, Somalia in 1993, Sudan in 1996, Yugoslavia in 1999, Afghanistan in 2001 and Iraq again in 2003) were mainly singled out because of their self-proclaimed independence. They were like the little neighborhood criminals who refuse to play along with the giant crime syndicates. The independents had considerably fewer weapons of mass destruction than the "compassionate imperialists" still have and were eliminated mostly because they were no longer following orders. Hussein was useful so long as he was trying to help the USA eliminate another nonconformist, the Iranian theocracy, but not when he tried to take over a country which was already conforming properly (Kuwait).

The same kind of reasoning also guided the Anglo-American counter-attacks against upstart empires in the First and the Second World Wars, as well as in the Cold War. Geopolitical hegemony was much more important in all of those situations than any ideological differences. Equally important was the Anglo-American attack on regimes which try to keep their national markets outside the "international community" of hegemonic investors. China and Japan had no more right to remain outside the world market during the nineteenth century than Nazi Germany, Soviet Russia, or Hussein's Iraq did later on. The Opium Wars (1839-1842, 1859-1860) and Commodore Perry's Japanese adventure (1854) are in that sense very similar to the 1990-1991 and 2003 campaigns against Iraq.

Meanwhile, this compassionate imperialism also includes the four or five million Congolese who have died since the beginning of Africa's "first world war", back in 1998. In that country, petroleum has been replaced by gold, diamonds and several other natural resources, with all of the Congo's neighbors participating in the so-called civil war. Apparently, the same division between Western powers that took place in Iraq also characterizes the neo-colonialism afoot in the Congo, with every local participant backed by a different consortium of Western governments and private investors.

Anglo-American compassionate imperialism means that the American and the British governments can do whatever they want, control however many countries and natural resources that they want, but other countries are not allowed to do the same. If the Russians or the Chinese or the Germans or the French try to do likewise, their imperialism is denounced as "naked aggression". If local dictators try to stand up to the Anglo-Americans, or if they try to cut deals with the middle powers, those competing efforts are denounced as idealism, pluralism, relativism and multilateralism. In fact, ever since the first division of the entire world into competing empires, back in 1885, the Anglo-American coalition has been desperately trying to prevent any other coalition of forces from challenging its hegemony.

However, it is also equally foolish for anyone on this planet to pretend that any of the competing empires, or any of the tin-pot dictators and terrorists from the Third World, are any better than the "compassionate" imperialists of the English-speaking world. This is why it is really stupid for all sorts of commentators to be constantly referring to terrorist events such as the September 11 massacre as being "inhuman". While these events are always extremely reactionary and disgusting, they are by no means inhuman. In fact, human beings, whether superpowers or tribal chieftains, have been indulging in this sort of thing, back and forth, ever since the first humanoids crawled out of Africa a couple of millions years ago!

Universal skeptics like us, therefore, do not harbor any illusions about our being able to change any of that, at least not right away. The world is set up in such a way that our scorn and our derision have no practical effect whatever either on the leaders of human institutions, or on the masses of the people who belong to those institutions. So terrorists will go on terrorizing, and governments will go on retaliating, and rapists will go on raping, regardless of what people like us may say about any of these situations. No one has so far devised any method of avoiding any of this, and all of those who claim that they have found "the way" are simply lying.

ISOLATED INCIDENTS

Why is it that practically every negative incident which ever took place in human society has always been officially isolated? Every time some deranged person, in some town or city, kills a large number of people, the mayor of that community always describes the incident as isolated. Every time someone is guilty of road rage, every time some killer assassinates an important personality, every time something or other goes very wrong in any public or private enterprise, every official whose responsibility is called into question, always comes up with the "isolated incident" gambit.

According to official reports, the assassination of JFK back in 1963 was an isolated incident, carried out by a lone gunman. So were the assassinations of Malcolm X, of Robert Kennedy, of Martin Luther King and of Jimmy Hoffa. In each one of those incidents, as well as hundreds of other such cases, the gunman is inevitably described as "lone" while the incident is always described as "isolated".

Another such incident took place in Quebec City in 1984, when another lone gunman entered the National Assembly and killed a bunch of people. In Montreal in 1989, another lone gunman killed 14 young women at the Ecole polytechnique. Several similar incidents take place almost once a week in the USA, the most well-known being the Columbine High School shootings of 1999. Similar shootings have also taken place in Germany recently, while in the year 2001, a lone gunman near Geneva, Switzerland, killed another group of lawmakers from a Swiss canton. Still another lonely individual was responsible for the July 4, 2002, incident at the Los Angeles airport, not to mention the even more recent assassination attempt on the president of France, or the sniper shootings in Washington, D.C. (In that last case, there were two "lone" gunmen.) For some strange reason, officials from each one of those places all talked about isolated incidents.

The laissez-faire government of Ontario also evoked the isolated incident theory to explain what happened in Walkerton, during the year 2000, when several people died because of the agricultural poisoning of that town's water supply. All the other towns in North America, Europe or anywhere else, in which similar events took place, were all treated as isolated incidents, which officials claim had nothing whatever to do with them, with government cut-backs in inspection services, or with any other group or service except perhaps that provided by the local community itself.

The Quebec government and its associated agencies reacted in exactly the same fashion to the 1996 floods in the Saguenay district and to the 1998 ice-storm; none of these "acts of God" ever had, or ever will have, any element whatsoever of human responsibility attached. At least, not according to any of the officials involved. The same scenario was played out once again in 2003, in China, and again in Ontario, in which the SARS epidemic was initially treated by laissez-faire governments in the same nonchalant way, at least before tourist revenues started to decline. In the meantime, no one has ever been able to convince Ontario, let alone voters for the Conservative Party's "common-sense revolution" against government intervention, that its do-nothing attitude toward health and the environment may have had something to do with the deaths in both Walkerton-2000 and Toronto-2003. As for China, communist totalitarianism does not seem to be any kind of bulwark against incompetence and indifference.

According to the Union Carbide Company, the poisoning of Bhopal, India, in 1984, was also an isolated incident. The now-defunct USSR claimed hundreds of such isolated incidents, including several thousand deaths in a nuclear accident in Siberia in 1958, as well as in the Chernobyl reactor explosion of 1986. The British government had the same opinion about its own nuclear accident, back in 1957, as did the American government when it lost an atomic bomb in the ocean off the coast of Spain. For the USA, even the 1947 "UFO" experiment in Roswell, New

Mexico, was just another isolated incident. Not to mention the 1989 sinking of the Exxon Valdez, or any of the other tanker sinkings. Needless to say, all of the world's mad-cow events, in Europe or in North America, were similarly isolated, or at least quarantined!

In fact, if we go back through recent history, even confining ourselves to events which took place only since 1945, we can come up with a list of several million "isolated" incidents, which have occurred in every part of the world. Every time anything at all goes wrong, if no natural cause can be found and if no organized group of bad guys claims responsibility, every person in power in the neighborhood of the incident always claims that it was isolated. Even the daily attacks on American soldiers in Iraq, after the fall of Saddam Hussein, are officially treated as isolated incidents!

In reality, of course, none of these incidents has ever been isolated. Every single official involved in these events, whether he or she was hired, appointed or elected to a position of responsibility, inevitably denied that responsibility whenever anything went wrong. These people were exactly like the extremely high-paid company executives who always claim all the credit whenever their companies do well, and who always blame someone else whenever their companies get into difficulty. No human being in power, no matter how well paid, ever acknowledges his or her responsibility for any disaster, unless forced to do so by others. The ritual acceptance of blame in Japan is no exception to this rule, since the ritualized nature of the act usually prevents the officials involved from actually serving any jail time for what they did.

This is why so many millions of these incidents end up being "isolated", some of them for a very long time. They are deliberately isolated from all the other incidents so as to minimize the negative impact on the people in charge, those who are extremely well-paid in order to be responsible, but who never seem to acknowledge that responsibility. In fact, all such incidents have all sorts of psychological and sociological relations with all sorts of other events. Political assassinations are invariably planned and carried out by large groups of people. Gunmen who burst into public or private buildings and shoot lots of people are always socially motivated: no human activity in world history could possibly exist without some social connection or another.

Government officials and company officials always use the isolated incident excuse in order to cover for their own incompetence. Every nuclear accident, every chemical accident, every mining accident, every water poisoning, every military experiment gone awry, every poorly-planned invasion, always involves some kind of official negligence. The same thing applies to most famines, as well as to shoddy construction in regions with lots of earthquakes or hurricanes. None of the egomaniacs who become well paid officials are ever capable of recognizing that fact, and blaming himself (or herself), without being forced into a confession.

The world is a social and collective place to live in, at all times. No gunmen are ever completely alone, no officials ever make entirely private decisions at work, and no incidents are ever totally isolated. All such people, and the events associated with their lives, are always sociologically connected. "No man is an island" (John Donne) and no "acts of God" have ever taken place in the real world entirely without human participation.

ONE BIG HAPPY FAMILY

The most important human institution of all, and the one which fails more often than all the others, is the family. This is an institution that has been around for millions of years, antedating such things as companies and governments. The main reason that it fails so often is exactly that: because it is more important, and has been around longer, than any of the other human groupings.

Families are organizations to which human individuals belong mainly for biological purposes. An adult human being may decide to join another family by getting married to someone within it, although that decision is still often made in more feudal societies by patriarchs and by matriarchs from over-extended families. An adult female may also decide to start a family, either by herself or in conjunction with a partner, usually a male partner, in the case of a nuclear family.

However, with the possible exception of equally powerless orphans who have not yet been adopted, the human child has to belong to a family over which he or she has no control whatsoever. This results in most individuals spending their entire lives dealing with people who are close to them because they are relatives, and not because they are friends. This situation seems ideally formulated so as to create an endless variety of problems, and is in fact the ultimate source of a great deal of human conflict.

Why in God's name would most of us want to live with some of the family members who inhabit almost everybody's family? It is a rare family indeed in which everyone loves everyone else and gets along with everyone else. Almost every claim concerning "one big happy family" turns out to be entirely bogus, invented for much the same ideological reasons that make some people believe in God, or democracy, or national greatness.

Much of the misery is generated by the fact that relatively powerless people, known as children, are obliged to live in the same dwelling as relatively powerful people, known as adults. In patriarchal families, everyone comes under the heel of a "Big Daddy", while in matriarchal families "Big Mommy" takes over the reins. On the other hand, in some other families, some of the children are occasionally allowed too much power, and end up ruining the lives of their parents and their lesser siblings. But in the majority of cases, relatively defenseless children suffer much more than do most of the adults.

Suffering usually becomes an inherited condition, which like weak knees is passed down from one generation to the next. As in many other human institutions, a person who is poorly treated as a child usually ends up poorly treating his own children as an adult. Physical and verbal abuses then become family characteristics, like patriotism or poverty, based on the brainless supposition that everyone else has to go through the same degradation that the original victim had to suffer.

One particularly telling aspect of all this human misery is the big family secret. Families with deep, dark secrets suffer as much, if not more so, than families within which the abuse is out in the open for everyone to see. The kinds of secrets that family members hide from each other are almost limitless, from membership in the Mafia to sexually transmitted diseases. All family members can play this game, but in most cases, the patriarch or the matriarch are the ones doing the hiding.

Children who find out about the Big Family Secret later on in life suffer in a number of different ways. Obviously, their respect for their parents is greatly reduced. If they find out at an early age, the almost religious worship of parents that most children engage in is seriously undermined. The child becomes upset not only about the original transgression, but also about the fact that the parent lied about it. If he or she can lie about that, what about all the other information concerning the family: is all that just a bunch of lies also?

One of the most traumatic discoveries a child can make is about his or her own status in the family. The most common scenario, and one of the most devastating, is for the child to find out that he or she is illegitimate, and does not really "belong" to one parent or the other. A lot of people react to this news by going off on a search for the missing biological parent, usually a deadbeat father. Actually finding the guy, and meeting him, may turn out to be more upsetting than not being able to do that. Discovering all kinds of half siblings all over the place is even more upsetting. All of that kind of thing turns a person's vision of the world upside down, and suddenly makes the planet a more dangerous place in which to live.

Some people's reaction to illegitimacy or to similar tales of woe from reconstituted families is to imagine that divorce and separation are inevitably worse than having the natural parents live together for life. But such is not the case. In fact, millions of children have been more traumatized from being forced to live with two people who hate each other, than with being forced to put up with a divorce, or a reconstituted family. Rotten parents are just as likely to be living together as they are to being divorced or separated.

No human society has yet stumbled upon a method of raising children which produces good results every time. Biological parents are often as useless or as harmful to their children, as are some foster parents. Extended families are most often even worse than nuclear families, since grandparents, aunts, uncles and so on are more often than not even more inclined than parents to harm children in some way or another, or to use them for various nefarious purposes. For example, most of the world's several hundred million slaves are under eighteen years of age, most of them working for nothing in extended-family enterprises. On the other hand, taking children away from the family altogether and raising them in some kind of political or social institution is usually even worse than the other methods.

It goes without saying that the children themselves are not always innocent people. There is nothing inherently innocent in the fact that a human being is under the legal age which defines an adult. Children have been known to commit all the major crimes as well as all the minor sins at whatever age they have to be in order to pick up a gun or a hammer. Nothing is more foolish than the fact that hundreds of thousands of children are allowed to get away with murder, among other things, merely because of their age. It comes under the same category ("ageism") as giving special privileges to other people just because they are older.

The whole situation is roughly analogous to what happens to minority groups such as the Black people in the USA, or what happens to Third World countries in a system dominated by economic empires. Groups of human beings who are weaker than other groups can justly blame the stronger groups for at least part of their problems. Individuals within those weaker groups, however, can be every bit as nasty as any of the individuals within the stronger groups. For example, a large part of the blame for the difficult situations in which Third World countries exist lies with many of the people from the Third World. The same thing goes for Black people in the USA, or for any other less powerful group. Children are in the same situation: as a group, they are weaker than adults, and therefore quite often exploited and brutalized. Individually, however, many children are as rotten as any of their adult dominators.

In permissive families, for example, spoiled-rotten children are not required to do anything at all, since the adults, mostly women, do all the housework, food preparation and so on. The same adults will often let their children brutalize them, either physically or verbally, in the same way that children are even more often brutalized in more traditional families. Children who act like little dictators do not do so because of their age, but because of their underlying personalities. Little Nazis are like big Nazis: the age difference is not at all fundamental.

The same types of problems continue to crop up even when the time comes for the children to leave their parents and to set out on their own. Some parents are either lazy or exasperated, and push their children out prematurely with little or no preparation. Others, just as egotistically, try to hold on to their children forever and actively encourage long-term dependency, since the parents themselves cannot bear to be "abandoned". The different kinds of abuse that I referred to earlier are then prolonged into adult life and transferred to yet another generation.

As with so many other, largely inadequate, human institutions, the family seems unavoidable. There are no "one big happy families", whether

Greek, Italian, East-Indian, or otherwise, and there are no ways to avoid living in an unhappy one. The best that we can hope for is to put up with a family that is not, after all, as bad as many other ones. The lesser evil strikes again!

FRENETIC FOLLIES

Another fascinating example of collective hysteria is speed psychosis. This disease can break out in any sector of the population, but it is usually more concentrated among young, aggressive males. The most well-known variety, at least in countries which depend a lot on the private automobile, is road mania. For some reason, people who have a lot of time on their hands and nowhere in particular to go are the ones who spend the most mental energy possible on driving about in a murderous rage. Even though their destination is of little importance to them, and they have nothing special to do when they get to that place, getting there quickly is somehow vital to their sense of well-being. The fact that they might be adding to the statistics on human road-kill while driving so fast will not slow them down; if anything, the danger involved only makes them go even faster. If they are going to kill someone, it might as well be worth it.

This particular psychosis has existed for as long as horses or mechanical vehicles have existed. The victims of this mental illness are mostly young males in heat, especially the ones who insist on driving motorcycles. These machines seem specifically to have been designed to kill, since their riders end up dead even more often than do the drivers of the other vehicles that they attack. The Neanderthals who ride them also enjoy the noise they make, which sounds even worse than a large animal breaking wind in public.

Several other varieties of speed psychosis are also well known. VIPs sometimes drive as fast as they can to prove to other people just how important they are, but most often they will order their chauffeurs to do the dirty work. Important people are particularly dangerous on the road because they know that they will never be punished if they hit anyone.

But speed does not just kill on the highway. Frenzied behavior has become a fact of life in several different places. Strobe-light entertainment has become the norm, particularly in popular culture. The ten-year-old kid mentality has taken over society, since every mall, every movie theater, and every dance floor, has to be inundated with rapidly changing colored lights, frantic and furious music and fake windstorms. Even movies shown to millions of captive adults on airplane flights are inevitably the kind of goofy action films that only young children could possibly enjoy. People seem to feel that they have to vomit, or at least to sport a throbbing headache, in order to prove that they are having fun.

One more place where frenzy has broken out is at work. For some unfathomable reason, people living in North America are being forced to work much longer hours now than they were twenty or thirty years ago. Overtime has become a fact of life for most of those who cannot simply clip investment coupons for a living. On the job, speed-up is still as important as it was when Taylorism was first invented back in the 1890s. Downsizing means that fewer people are expected to do the work of many, with no corresponding changes in the work set-up.

Sycophants enjoy providing some sort of justification for this variety of madness. They say that a lot of this activity is necessary since society needs quite a few over-achievers in order to provide all the wealth and the discoveries and the efficiencies that fast people have a habit of introducing. According to this argument, if everyone just sat back and enjoyed the good life, there would not be nearly enough material progress being made to ensure everyone's survival.

The truth is that all of this enforced efficiency and longer hours only result in speculators having more of other people's money to waste. The apologists seem to have forgotten that most of this frenzied activity is wasted, since every gang of go-getters is out there undoing all the work of every other gang. Every publicity company is trying to outdo every other publicity company, with the only end result being the sale of a lot of worthless junk to people who do not need most of what they buy. Every pro-abortion demonstration is countered with every anti-abortion assassination attempt and every peace movement is countered by every "silent majority".

At every stage of the game, the Enron (World-Com) Limit-Breaking Society burns ordinary people up, to provide dishonest brokers with junk-bond entertainment. Wasting other people's lives on the futures market is even more fun than running over someone on the highway. Activity for activity's sake works the same way as any other drug, providing frenzied people with the fix that they need so that they will hopefully never notice the emptiness of their stupid little lives.

All over the world, workaholics try to hold down several jobs at a time, while simultaneously embarking on all sorts of extra-curricular projects. Superwomen try to prove their new-found equality by raising several children, usually all by themselves, working impossible hours and still insisting on going on three or four frenetic vacations per year. Needless to say, these over-achievers never do their work well, since they are always obliged to cut corners in order to get everything done. Botched work, botched lives and botched children are the inevitable result. Somehow, many of these people still manage to win prizes and publicity as pillars of the community and examples of excellence.

Needless to say, amphetamines, appropriately called speed, and a host of other performance drugs have also taken over the antediluvian world of sports. Racing car drivers from the old days have been joined by a psychotic mob of Olympic proportions, driven by the speed-worship of the Summer Games and the Winter Games. Athletes and governments all over the world are always trying to conceal their own dope-taking, all the while hypocritically denouncing other people's dope-taking. If there are no Olympics coming up in any particular sport for the next six months, people invent Special Events to replace them. Thousands of young devils have to be skating or wrestling to their doom in order to entertain billions of couch potatoes watching at home.

Unfortunately, if the writers of any one of a number of recent, science-fiction movies can be believed, this is one more problem which is not going to disappear any time soon. No matter how fast the frenetic people may go, they will never be able to catch up to whatever remains of their own ruined lives. Only by taking the time to look around and reflect on what exactly is taking place can anyone ever discover anything important.

MINORITY OF ONE

Many of the people who commented on the contents of my first book of skepticism objected to the fact that I do not seem to want to be part of the real world. For them, my rejection of all extant religions and ideologies, in every area of human endeavor, is both impossible and egotistical. They say that everyone has to take sides in every conflict and that no one is so good that he or she can exclude himself, or herself, from the decisions being made every day in society. In their opinion, everyone is capable of evil, even great evil, and anyone's pretension to be above all that is just nonsense.

In fact, I could not agree more. During the writing of my first book, I paid more than just lip service to the idea that a total absence of ideology is impossible among human beings. I also have an ideology of sorts, hidden behind all of my attacks on competing ideologies. But I do not revel in that shortcoming, nor do I try to turn it into something positive like both the true believers and the unconscious hypocrites try to do.

The real original sin is that by having a particular point of view, we are eventually forced to lie about something or other which that point of view does not really cover. By trying to extend our theory beyond the breaking point, we end up falling into the same trap which we originally denounced, in someone else's thinking. At the same time, all humans are obliged to have a particular point of view anyway. No one can even start to think about anything without relating his or her thoughts to some particular, and therefore ultimately incorrect, point of view.

Today's neo-conservative ideology has gone further than most, however, by elevating lying into a universal art form. Lowest-common denominator publicity has carpeted the entire Earth with systematic lying, replacing fascist or communist propaganda with a much more effective manner of hiding the truth. People in relatively democratic countries may think that they are being manipulated less than people in obviously totalitarian countries, but in reality intelligent lying has simply replaced the more primitive kinds. So, even though everyone has to fall short of the absolute truth all of the time, the neo-cons have turned propaganda into a virtue; their entire system of values is based on it.

This is why it is so amusing, or so pathetic, to realize that many people voted for neo-conservative politicians like George Bush the Second because they felt that those politicians were more honest than the others, that they "tell it like it is". Unfortunately, ignorant people still equate populist pretensions with the truth, as if "sounding just like us" had something to do with being straightforward. They do not seem to be able to deal with the fact that anyone in a position of power, such as a serious candidate for the leadership of an important country like the USA, could not possibly get nominated, let alone get elected, if that person ever told the truth for any reason. All over the world, populist leaders, not just of countries but also of companies and of trade unions, always turn out to be even more dishonest than leaders who openly despise powerless people.

In order to avoid this kind of deliberate lying, skeptics still have to rely on the scientific method, particularly in the social sciences such as history. No good scientist nowadays claims any longer that he or she can really achieve a total absence of prejudice and bias, at any time. The goal, however, is still to try to get as far away from ideology as possible and to let it influence scientific work as little as possible. Even though scientists realize that all facts are ideological constructs, they still feel that trying to get as close to the truth as possible is better than trying to keep as far away from it as possible, by deliberately believing in something in particular.

The scientific outlook is built up by starting with raw data, facts and figures, which are accumulated after much theory-based observation and experiment. The raw data is supposed to suggest a hypothesis, some inductive or deductive idea which attempts to make sense of that particular set of information. Several hypotheses are then brought together to make

105

a concept, several concepts are brought together to make a theory, several theories are brought together to make a doctrine and similar doctrines end up as a general ideology. Armed with particular points of view, scientists then go out and collect even more so-called raw data, and the process starts all over again.

Most scientists like to think that they can avoid doctrines and ideologies altogether, and so they end up talking about paradigms instead. But paradigms, as Thomas Kuhn and dozens of other thinkers have pointed out, are just doctrines and ideologies disguised as science. Science is a much better source of knowledge than tradition, or religion or any other kind of thinking, but only because it makes a conscious effort at doing away with any ideas which cannot be related to observation and experiment in the real world. Nevertheless, science cannot dispense with ideological thinking completely, since no one ever has all the answers to all the questions.

Only religious believers, political fanatics and insane people think that they know everything, because they have lost the ability to distinguish between reality and fantasy. Religious and ideological exaggeration makes these people think that part of reality can be extended to cover all of it.

In the discipline of history, for example, almost everyone now agrees that it is impossible to reconstruct the past exactly as it was. But that does not mean that historians have to let current trends and biases unduly color their vision of the past. They have to try and get as close as they possibly can to how the people of days gone by were thinking at the time that they were living their lives. Quite often, their approach was considerably different from current ways of thinking, and therefore is extremely difficult to understand nowadays.

When history is treated as a science instead of as a heritage, the accent is on trying to find out the truth, at least insofar as that is possible, rather than on trying to glorify current institutions. People who think about the past seriously realize that the "good old days" never existed anywhere and that most people back then, like most people nowadays, were not kings and princesses, but slaves and rape victims.

In the same way, when people try to understand something that is going on in the present, it does no good whatsoever to make an investigation without first attempting to rid ourselves of whatever prejudices are currently popular. Pretending that we are outside of the universe, looking in, is the only way that we can put enough distance between ourselves and our object of study, so as to make that study meaningful. So what if the results do not support whatever normative advice that preachers and proselytizers would like to be handing out to the people involved?

Sure most of us have to do our jobs in order to survive, which means that we have to participate in local decision-making. Nothing in that everyday process, however, requires us to leave our brains in the toilet bowl when it comes to understanding what is going on around us. Just because everyone has to participate in society in order to live does not mean that any of us have to agree with whatever it is that is going on, even if we happened to be present when some of the stupid decisions were being made.

Those of us who live in democratic societies, for example, are not obliged to go out and vote every so often, just because the voting system is better than dictatorship. None of us really have to hold our noses and vote for some particular politician rather than another, and then to feel guilty later on when that yokel inevitably makes some ignorant decision that we do not agree with whatsoever. Everyone knows, or ought to know, that the plutocrats control democratic societies every bit as much as they control their favorite military dictators.

One of the most interesting recent examples of that problem was in the 2002 presidential elections in France. In the first round, millions of voters stayed at home because they were unwilling to choose between an exceptionally corrupt conservative politician and a particularly inept socialist politician. As it turned out, this resulted in the dark horse, ultra-nationalist candidate coming second in the presidential race. For the first time since the Second World War, a neo-fascist candidate had a shot at becoming the first elected neo-Nazi in French history. To prevent that from happening, millions of normally socialist voters then helped elect the corrupt conservative instead. In other words, instead of helping people choose a better life, the French electoral system made them "choose" someone who only received twenty percent of the free vote (the first one).

But it is no fun at all to stay within the structure and to participate in whatever kinds of horrors that are currently being perpetrated. It contributes nothing to humanity to help the toxic personalities succeed with their nefarious little stratagems for gaining ever more power and influence. Sharing the blame, covering our tracks, hiding the truth from others, who needs it?

It makes no sense whatever to get involved in social decision-making as though some kind of national or international consensus were genuinely possible. For example, commentators in several countries are currently upset at many of today's university students because they refuse to get their feet wet and to take sides in any of the great issues of the moment. According to these sycophants, democracy is suffering because lots of people refuse to take a stand for or against any particular policy.

But this sort of objection assumes that some kind of consensus building process is in fact possible. In reality, however, the rulers rule without requiring anyone else to take a stand. As I pointed out in my first book, they make their decisions for all sorts of reasons which are not at all related to the best interests of the majority of people, in plutocratic democracies or anywhere else. The consensuses that they so eagerly seek are designed to let them rule over powerless people with impunity, not to actually carry out any particular policy decision.

In addition, it does no good whatever to assume that other people would make as poor decisions as the world's leaders do, if they were in their shoes. It helps nothing to say that ordinary (powerless) people are just as bad as their chieftains, or that all human beings are equally capable of evil. The fact remains that murderers most often get longer prison sentences than do counterfeiters, and that jaywalking is not considered to be as serious a crime as genocide.

This is why the often-quoted statement from British writer H. G. Wells, to the effect that "moral indignation is jealousy with a halo", is so dangerous. Those who firmly believe in the lesser evil use the dismissal of moral indignation as a way of covering their tracks. Any sort of disgusting behavior becomes perfectly acceptable when someone argues that all those who despise that behavior are just jealous morons, who wish that they were capable of as much evil as the original perpetrators. Getting upset about anything, from full-blown genocide on down to indecent exposure in a public park, is therefore easily ignored, since everyone would presumably have done the same had he or she only been capable of it!

Whenever someone gets sufficiently indignant with all of the politicians, or all of the perpetrators of whatever sort of anti-social behavior, the legions of apologists are always called upon. The spin-doctors and the hired publicists then proclaim that everyone should simply hold his nose and vote for someone, anyone, because apathy only leads to totalitarianism. The same sort of thing also happens outside politics, like when those who work for some private enterprise are told that they cannot afford to get upset at the company owner, because he or she has "provided" them with their jobs. Another example is when poor countries are told that they have no right to criticize rotten job conditions in some multinational company's factory because after all the wages paid by the giant corporation are so much higher than those paid by local firms.

Similarly, the ideologues will not allow anyone to remain neutral in the fight between dominant countries and the Moslem extremists because those extremists inevitably blow up innocent civilians regardless of whether or not the victims were self-proclaimed neutrals. It does not seem to have occurred to the apologists that the dominant countries also regularly kill innocent civilians, in larger numbers than the Moslem terrorists have so far been capable of doing.

Take another frequent occurrence. How many times have innocent people been caught in the wrong place at the wrong time when some kind of violent demonstration takes place? A large group of people demonstrating against globalization, for example, often becomes violent, either because anarchist elements within the crowd planned on violence, or because police agents among the demonstrators start getting violent in order to justify a large-scale assault on what had been, up until then, a peaceful demonstration. Once the over-wrought police force runs amok and starts charging the demonstrators in every direction, hundreds of innocent bystanders are often killed, or badly hurt, because they were going about their normal affairs in a place which happened to be over-run by the demonstrators and the accompanying riot squad.

What is the difference between the innocent bystanders caught between anarchists and anti-anarchists, the same bystanders caught between terrorists and anti-terrorists, and the same bystanders once again caught between corrupt mainstream politicians and just-as-corrupt neo-Nazi politicians? In every case, innocent people are getting clobbered by guilty people. Those who do not want to take part in evil are being forced to participate, often in the worst possible ways.

The innocent bystander, the person who does not want to choose between Hitler and Stalin, or between a totalitarian God and an anarchist Devil, or this kind of evil versus that kind of evil, is invisible in human society. He or she is constantly being trampled back and forth by the takers-of-sides. A person blessed with the kind of moral indignation which renders him or her relatively immune to the collective hysteria of partisanship, who desperately wants to avoid making one kind of terrible mistake (or another kind), never has his opinion consulted. None of the belongers from this side or that side want to hear from the non-participant, none of them are at all interested in finding out that all of their teams are in fact morally disqualified. Conscientious objectors are always hated by everyone who stands in line, waiting his turn to kill or be killed.

The innocent bystander does not want to participate because he feels no common ground with any of the current contenders. But even when he represents the majority of all the human beings in any given situation, he is always ignored, since his point of view, deliberately rejecting all of the committed points of view on any subject, is unacceptable to those who choose to fight. The innocent bystander feels left out and impotent, unable to change the way people do things, since taking sides, team spirit, is all and everything. The belongers go to unbelievable lengths to protect their own contributions to the fight, and their own institutional righteousness. The innocent bystander can never be allowed to jeopardize society, even civilization itself, by pointing out the obvious: that the esprit de corps of the institution is itself everyone's main enemy.

It is the very conflict itself which distorts reality. Whether someone upholds some social institution, or wants to replace that institution with another one, makes no difference. It is the very holding of an opinion about that institution, for or against, which is the source of misunderstanding, since it results in one kind of distortion or another. Bush versus Saddam Hussein or bin Laden, Israel versus Palestine, the

World Trade Organization versus the anarchist coalition, none of those partisan points of view are capable of seeing the world for what it is. Once again, however, this does not mean that any of those institutions are equally good or bad.

This is where a lot of intolerance comes from, when committed people refuse to tolerate the very existence of the uncommitted. Their attitude is analogous to that of true believers in any of the revealed religions. Among other things, religious believers find it intolerable to realize that human beings are not special at all, but just so many specks in an infinite universe. They become extremely upset when they are told that things happening on the surface of this planet do not seem to be so terribly important in the universal scheme of things.

Unfortunately for them, it seems that in the real universe, any small portion of infinity is still infinite by itself. So the chances are good that a very large number of planets with intelligent life on them do exist, besides our own, making what happens here relatively insignificant. This is probably true whether or not the available evidence supports a one Big-Bang universe, an alternating Big-Bang-Big-Crunch sequence, a universe dominated by dark matter or a multiple-universe scenario.

I find that the intolerance that such religious believers feel toward the infinite universe is analogous to the intolerance that secular believers, otherwise known as committed people, feel toward the politically uncommitted. People, who believe wholeheartedly in democracy or the superiority of their own country over all the others, or whatever other idea is currently popular, get really upset when they are told that their political beliefs are worthless. Their rage and their intolerance, however, do not make that irrelevance any less real. Democracy, or any other political idea, does not work well simply because a relatively large number of people have decided to believe in it. Wishing will not make it so.

Patriotism is probably the worst example of organized intolerance. The self-righteousness of patriotic people makes them tolerate all sorts of disgusting behavior on the part of their country's rulers, while simultaneously making them exceptionally intolerant of the actions of other countries! In fact, patriotism is an immoral disease, similar to cheating on one's spouse, or driving too fast in a school zone, or gambling, or low sales resistance. It indicates more than any other belief that the practitioner is a simpleton, someone who cannot resist the temptation to be and act like everyone else who lives in the same neighborhood.

In my opinion, all these forms of intolerance are also analogous to the way that toxic personalities react when one of their victims tries to complain to them about their disgusting behavior. Instantly, their hackles go up and they become incapable of hearing, much less comprehending any criticism whatsoever. For a toxic personality, the victim's bleating is as intolerable as skepticism is to a true believer, religious or political.

Luckily for such believers, the impact of books like this one is not all that great. People seem to have an infinite capacity for continuing to believe in whatever they like to believe, regardless of how many different books are written denouncing that fact. It also does not seem to make any difference if critical books, or critical messages of any kind, are commercial flops or commercial success stories. The capacity of believers to go on believing, regardless of everything, seems to be as infinite as anything else which exists anywhere in the universe.

TELLING THE TRUTH ABOUT HISTORIOGRAPHY

One of the more useful books to have been published during the last decade of the twentieth century was "Telling the Truth about History", written by a trio of feminist historians in the USA: Joyce Appleby, Lynn Hunt and Margaret Jacob. This was a book about Western historiography since the Second World War, about how Americans and other Westerners have been interpreting world history over the past several decades. The authors dealt with the difference between science and ideology in the writing of history in a relatively intelligent way, while still managing to avoid what ought to have been their main point.

Over and over again, they referred to such things as the absolutist image of positivist science, or science as the guarantor of progress and power, or the compatibility between nationalism and science in early American history, or the attempt to combine the closest possible approach to truth with the struggle for a more intellectually alive and democratic society. In every one of these images, it never seems to have occurred to those historians that science is not capable of being combined with any other goals, and still remain scientific.

In order for science to be science, whether in the writing of history or any other scientific endeavor, the scientist has to do whatever he or she can do to free his or her work from any sort of ideological bias. In spite of the fact that that was precisely what the authors' intention seems to have been in writing their book, they persisted in thinking that science could be tied to some other goal and still remain science.

Unfortunately, that is not possible. Science cannot be absolutist or democratic, or tied to any other ideology, without ceasing to be scientific. In my first book, I showed that any attempt to use science in any particular way cannot be compatible with science. Even though it is impossible for any human being to cut himself or herself off from the society from which he or she springs, that attempt must still be made.

Throughout their entire book, the authors refer both, on the one hand, to the kind of positivist science which supposedly upholds Western imperialism, democracy and the free market, and on the other hand to the attacks on all knowledge having been carried out by relativist thinkers like Jacques Derrida and Michel Foucault. According to Appleby, Hunt and Jacob, both positivist and relativist ways of thinking are necessarily suspect because both are tied nevertheless to Western values. They even went so far as to compare William Jennings Bryan's Christian-fundamentalist attack on social Darwinism, to recent relativist attacks on Western science as if it caused Hiroshima and the danger of all-out nuclear war.

But attacking science for causing social Darwinism and the bombing of Hiroshima is like attacking Black people for slavery, by blaming the victim for the crime. Just because scientific discoveries can be used in order to kill or to enslave others does not mean that science has to be rejected, or that we have to adopt the relativists' conceit that all forms of knowledge are as good as science. The word "science" simply means the kind of thinking which takes place when intelligent people attempt to expand upon and organize useful information about anything or anybody, using the most value-free methods available.

As the authors point out, science is not the same as logical positivism, nor is it properly defined by Karl Popper's metaphysical realism. Scientific revolutions and paradigms are ideological constructs, after all, even though that does not mean that science has to be rejected for its prejudices. A "scientific" prejudice is simply that which is left over even after an entire community of sharp minds has made every possible effort to remove every possible bias. There is in fact nothing identifiable in a scientific effort that can be successfully attacked by relativists as grounds for dismissal.

Making a connection between science and progress, as the authors so often do, is not the same. Progress is most often used as an identifiable ideological construct and as such has no business being associated with science. In my first book, I explained that even though it may be possible to identify some sort of progress in human civilization, just by the very fact that a much larger number of humans are currently alive than used to be the case, this does not mean much. The kinds of progress that most people refer to when they use this word, such as more material well-being or greater degrees of democracy, are not universally evident, nor proven.

The authors of this important book have been thrown off by their equation between relativism and skepticism, which they see as being synonyms. Skepticism, however, is a real synonym for science, but not for relativism. A relativist thinks that all forms of knowledge are equal, that all kinds of society are morally equivalent, and that religious thinking is no worse than rational thinking. The authors themselves indulged in this kind of relativism when they denounced Darwin's atheism and materialism as simply forms of religion. In reality, Darwin made mistakes in his theory of evolution not because of his atheism or materialism, but because of his reliance on Malthusian economic theories as the source of his theory about the survival of the fittest. Darwin erred not because of his objectivity toward a non-existent God, but because of his lack of social objectivity toward the so-called inferior classes of society.

Skepticism is not like relativism. A skeptic is simply someone who thinks scientifically as often as he or she possibly can. It is a person who can accept all sorts of propositions temporarily, if he or she is convinced of their temporary superiority over other interpretations, at least until some better explanation comes along. Such a person will not reject a proposition simply because its proponents claim that it is better than another proposition, like the relativists do. Skeptics and scientists deal in terms of inferior and superior propositions all the time. They try to find real reasons for choosing one proposition over another, rather than simply rejecting the whole lot as being equally ideological.

The authors' attempt at being scientific fell short of its goal for the same reason that they themselves were capable of criticizing Newton's theory of gravitation, because of its inspiration from Newton's belief in God. In fact, Appleby, Hunt and Jacob have about the same problem as Newton had because of their belief in "America", or US nationalism.

115

Even as revisionist historians, they are as incapable of escaping from their American ideological prison and at least trying to become citizens of the world, as Newton was incapable of rejecting God. Unfortunately for them, the attempt to escape one's national origins is also an integral part of the attempt at being scientific.

These historians are justified in their attack on the postmodern rejection of all history-writing as being as ideological as magic or religion, but their own meta-narrative program for creating a more intellectually alive and democratic society defeats their purpose. Unfortunately, the search for any particular social paradigm, or practical reason, is not part of science. Science has to be skeptical of democratic society for the same reason that is has to be skeptical of logical positivism, or of post-structural relativism: any social or political program whatsoever is inimical to science.

This fact should be particularly evident to historians, who are specifically engaged in discovering the roots of all current reality. Appropriately, the authors cite Pieter Geyl's observation that all history is an interim report, but they themselves do not seem to completely understand all of the consequences of such a statement. History is an interim report because life is an interim report, as is science, which tries to reflect life as simply as possible, through the intelligent use of Ockham's razor (the simplest hypothesis possible). Since there are no final conclusions to be made about anything, no particular project is worthy of scientific support.

To be genuinely scientific, rational inquiry has to imitate the old MGM slogan about art: "Ars gratia artis", art for art's sake. The craving for insight into what it means to be human, to which the authors refer, can only give relatively objective results (the pun is intended) if it is based on a constantly renewed desire to avoid all normative goals. While it is true that objects do not accommodate all possible interpretations, and therefore that science is possible, this can only come about if the intellectual demand for accuracy is divorced from the soul's desire for metaphysical meaning. A shared commitment to objective knowledge has to be predicated on the rejection of science as a form of virtuous living, or any other extension.

The democratic practices of the USA or any other country can never arrive at any common goals precisely because of the overwhelming influence of well-financed interest groups within those countries. The authors are living in a fantasy world if they genuinely believe that Americanism is synonymous with democracy in any absolute sense. They are as wrong as was the 1940s leader of the Communist Party in the USA, Earl K. Browder, when he claimed that communism was twentieth-century Americanism. While telling the truth is indeed a collective effort, the structure which can bring that about is a universal republic of learning, loosely-defined, and not a republic in the classic sense, like France or the USA. Even the most democratic republics in the real world will only tolerate free scientific inquiry to a limited extent. Pretending otherwise is simply another form of myth-making.

Instead, historians and history teachers should be joining with other scientists, other educators and other skeptics (the republic of learning), all over the world, in the expansion and dissemination of science for science' sake. New discoveries and old ones have to be transmitted to as many other people as possible, without getting bogged down in the quagmires of either parochial or relativist ideology. Courses have to be taught which are centered on taboo-free comparisons between different cultures and periods, and on the process of acquiring knowledge rather than on the current paradigms. Students should not be allowed to finish a course without having to reflect on their own learning process (metacognition) and on the very real differences between the signified object and the subjective signifier. Telling the truth about history also includes telling the truth about historiography.

Such goals can never be fully achieved, but making the attempt (asymptotic convergence, to use a mathematical analogy) is the only social objective worthy of its name.

HISTORY VERSUS HERITAGE

This is why it is so important to properly distinguish between history and heritage, between trying to find out what really happened in the past and what ideologically-minded people would have liked to have happened in the past. Every country, as well as every religion and every ideology, always invents its own myths to explain its origins, oftentimes cleverly based on real events. Those mythologies are then projected onto the present and believed in as if they were real.

The scholarly work which seems to have contributed the most to our understanding of this process is David Lowenthal's book, "Possessed by the Past: The Heritage Crusade and the Spoils of History". In that book, published in 1996, Lowenthal presented an incredibly large number of cases of historical deformations, showing equally well that the official pronouncements of traditional heritage-mongers were only slightly more off-base than the competing claims of the politically correct. According to Lowenthal, every country in the world has invented a whole series of mythical "founding fathers" to replace the real ones, who were never as brave, as democratic, or as visionary as today's patriots require them to be. Even the anti-communists in the USA, while pretending to worship the Constitution, regularly denounce several of its principles.

Lowenthal also pointed out that historical faking remains potent in most societies long after the fakery has been demolished by professional historians, and even long after the deception was admitted by institutional authorities. Cases in point that he cited include the "donation of Constantine", a fake document written by monks in the Middle Ages which was supposed to have shown how the Christian emperor Constantine passed on the mantle of Jesus Christ to the Catholic Popes. Even though everyone, including the Catholic Church, now admits that this document was a fraud, the world's 900 million Catholics still go on believing in some kind of direct, two millennia long passage of power from Saint Peter to John Paul II. According to Lowenthal, the same current potency also applies to the "Protocols of the Elders of Zion", a nineteenth-century Russian fake about Jewish intentions for taking over the world which is still being cited as "evidence" by anti-Semites in the Middle East.

In the same tradition is an even more recent book ("Historical Taboos") by the prolific French historian Marc Ferro, whose works are often translated into several other languages. It seems that Ferro got the idea for writing this particular book over twenty years ago, when he unsuccessfully tried to convince a French audience that Joan of Arc was in fact a lesbian. Apparently, although the available evidence seems to support it, that idea did not go over very well in France, even in radical circles. Another even more fascinating case investigated by Ferro was the orthodox-Jewish claim about the Hebraic origins of most of today's Jews. In fact, it turns out that since Judaism has sometimes indulged in conversion and even mass conversion (though not nearly so often as Christianity did), the majority of today's Jews could not possibly trace their origins to the Biblical Middle East.

According to Ferro, the most important of such conversions involved the wholesale transformation of the nomadic Khazar tribes from the plains of Eastern Europe into the Jewish religion during the ninth century. Such a massive event, at least in comparison to the overall numbers of the world's Jews, along with similar conversions in many other areas on a smaller scale, further undermines the Zionist claim to Palestine, or Israel.

This does not, however, reinforce the Palestinian-Arab claim to the same region, since the Arabs did not arrive in that region any earlier than the ancient Hebrews did, nor are the Arabs any more homogenous than the world's Jews.

Even the Old Testament shows that the Hebrews were not the first people to occupy that part of the eastern Mediterranean, but the fact that most of today's Jews are not even related to the Hebrews underlines just how foolish that claim really is. It also forces a reinterpretation of the related claim that Jews are "God's chosen people", which is used by

119

fundamentalist Christians as well as by Zionists to support everything now being done by the state of Israel.

This obviously has its importance in current world politics. The fact is that first occupation of territory is an extremely difficult thing to prove, especially since archeologists are always coming up with new finds all over the world. A still more important reality is that no group of human beings should be able to claim exclusive rights over any particular territory no matter how long their ancestors may have inhabited the region. In spite of everything, however, millions of people still feel that their own identifies are defined by their adhesion to some particular piece of geography.

The "First Nations", or Amerindians of North America, are particularly adept at doing this, with some ethnic groups going so far as to prevent scientists from investigating ancient skeletons, in case they turn up politically unacceptable evidence. No one wants to admit that the reburial of ancient skeletons for religious or ethnic purposes is every bit as racist as digging those skeletons out in order to uphold racial stereotypes. Most people still do not realize that indigenous peoples are just as potentially racist as imperialist peoples. All that the "nativists" want to prove is their own racial legitimacy by claiming some particular piece of land as their own.

Among such ethnic or religious taboos, the writing of many of humanity's most sacred texts is probably the most important. The Christian Bible, for example, is a compendium of several different works, including thousands of contradictory elements, and written by hundreds of different people, both in the Jewish section (the Old Testament) and in the Christian section (the New Testament). Several of the books which compose the Bible are in dispute, with different groups (both Christian and Jewish) claiming that different works are, or are not, to be included among the sacred texts. The authors of many of those works are also in dispute, since several texts seem to be have been written by various different people at various times. Even the four most commonly accepted Christian gospels were obviously written by people who did not have any first-hand experience with the events being described and were only interested in using those events for some sectarian purpose. As a result, almost every part of the Bible is incremental, and could certainly not have been written that way under the influence of any perfect being.

The same type of analysis can also be made for every other sacred text on this planet. The Moslem Koran, for example, contains almost as many internal contradictions as the Bible, and also seems to have been written in an incremental way, by many different people over a period of several centuries. In these cases, as well as in many others, the official, sacred versions of events are in fact light-years away from historical truth.

Another interesting myth or taboo is the "Third World" ideology's contention that all or most of today's problems in Asian, African and Latin American countries are direct consequences of the Western empires' colonization process. A group of about twenty French authors, including Marc Ferro again, have published another recent work, "The Black Book of Colonialism", in which they freely admit that Third World countries were very poorly treated during the colonial period. They even go so far as to underline that the deaths of about 50 million Amerindians in both North and South America during early colonization were not just caused by the unfortunate importation of Old World diseases, which killed off most of the American Indians by accident. It seems that in most cases, the Spanish, the Portuguese, the English, the French and several other European colonial nations deliberately encouraged the spread of such diseases and sufficiently weakened the local populations through early attempts at indigenous slavery so that they died off much more rapidly than they otherwise would have.

However, the same historians also show that the transport of millions of African slaves to the Americas, to replace the dead Amerindians, was not such a new thing after all. Not only had African kings sold their prisoners of war to traders from various Ancient and Medieval empires, for several centuries prior to European expansion, and not only were Europeans themselves often enslaved by North African and Western Asian empires up through to the twentieth century. It seems that Arab-speaking traders also continued the slave trade through to the latter part of the twentieth century, selling African slaves illegally to Europeans and Americans even after the slave trade was officially abolished in the Western empires. It also turns out that even during the colonial period, Western slave-traders only bought as many slaves as the Arab traders did.

In other words, human slavery has never been exclusively or even mainly a creature of Western imperialism, as the Third World apologists had claimed during the last half of the twentieth century. This is further underlined by today's slave trade which, although illegal all over the planet, still thrives everywhere. Hundreds of millions of slaves, mostly women and children, are still working for no salary in various different regions, most notably in Asia, which may only have the greatest number of slaves because it has the largest proportion of the entire human population.

Rich people in North America, Western Europe and the Middle East are also still very much involved in today's slave trade, based on such groups as Eastern European prostitutes and Filipino domestic servants. In Montreal recently, one newspaper was forced to pull an advertisement for Filipino servants being offered to rich households by a local immigration agency. It seems that 800 Canadian dollars was the going price for a live-in domestic servant, unaware of her rights in Canadian society!

Still another fascinating taboo concerns the active collaboration between capitalists and socialists to exploit the colonial world, ever since modern imperialism began during the 1880s. Most textbooks completely ignore the important role of farmer-labor Progressivism and democratic socialism in supporting ordinary capitalist empires. The same textbooks also treat communist empires as if they were somehow different from capitalist empires. Fascism in Italy, Germany and a hundred other countries is still presented as if it too were not simply part of a greater alliance of capitalist and socialist forces spanning the entire twentieth century.

But the fascist and the communist empires of the twentieth century were all just radical versions of the modern imperialist control of the entire world, starting in 1884-1885 (the Congress of Berlin). The rulers of empires which were too weak to survive the First World War used those socialistic ideologies to try to wrest hegemony away from the liberal empires that won that war. As I pointed out in my first book, however, all of the totalitarian powers simply substituted state capitalism for private capitalism to greater or lesser degrees. None of them actually tried to change the rules of the game in any significant way. Even their temporary seizure of new colonies, in both Europe and the Third World, were only aggressions in imitation of what larger liberal empires (Britain, France and the USA) had already accomplished beforehand. Stalin himself best summed up the overall social-imperial attitude toward ideas when commenting on the influence of religion on politics: "How many troops does the Pope have?"

The Progressive movements of the 1880-1920 period in the USA and the UK, most of the more moderate socialist and social-democratic parties in several other countries since that time, as well as most of the communist parties, actively supported most of the colonial adventures undertaken in the name of market expansion and national prestige. Racism, nativism, anti-Semitism and eugenics were very much a part of all those populist movements, along with the more frequently analyzed characteristics such as free-silver, free-trade, opposition to monopoly and oligopoly, support for trade unions and farmers' cooperatives, and so on.

British historian Bernard Semmel best described the process by which the leading imperialists of the early twentieth century joined up with the representatives of Lenin's "labor aristocracy" to found social-imperialism. This same social-imperialism has since cropped up in several different disguises, uniting most of the liberal, conservative, socialist, fascist and communist parties into one large block of colonialist and neo-colonialist domination. Seen from the Third World, the political differences between all those different parties seem relatively unimportant.

In fact, heritage blunders of this sort cover the entire gamut of religious and secular ideologies. Every group of human beings, in every country or region, and in every generation, always invents erroneous interpretations of history as a shared mythology. Such inventions are always extremely important to the groups involved and influence every decision that people make even in their day-to-day, practical existence.

For example, actor Susan Sarandon, one of the victims of the recent war mania in the USA, found it ironic that the USA was attacking Iraq for its lack of democracy, while simultaneously trying to silence its own citizens who were opposed to the war. Such an event, however, is not ironic, but merely par for the course. None of the historically based ideas which people believe in are actually supposed to be taken at face value.

As the well-known anarchist writer in Montreal, Pierre Foglia has pointed out democracy has become just another religion. People are not supposed to actually test the historical content of democracy, to see whether or not it really represents what it is supposed to represent. They are just supposed to believe in it as a heritage, as a kind of cohesive slogan which can be used to help keep the group that a person belongs to from falling apart. When people claimed that all truly democratic countries were obliged to participate in the wars against Saddam Hussein, it was not really democracy as a political system that they were talking about. They were not interested in upholding the genuine content of the ideas contained in democratic documents from the past like the Declaration of the Rights of Man or the United States Constitution.

What they really wanted to do was to use democratic ideals as a symbol in order to rally as many people as possible around the flag, more or less in the same way that Saddam Hussein used Middle Eastern leaders from the past like Saladin or Nebuchadnezzar as symbols to buttress his own dictatorship. The actual content of democracy, such as of letting people continue to enjoy freedom of speech even in wartime, is not what the warmongers meant when they talked about democracy. What they meant was that democracy, human rights and the US Constitution should be used as propaganda slogans to get people to support Anglo-American control of the Middle East and its natural resources, or whatever other practical goals happened to be on their agenda at that time.

In the same manner, Christians and Moslems the world over have freely supported laissez-faire capitalism even though its principles are diametrically opposed to the stated principles of the Christian and Moslem religions. Likewise, Catholic priests all over the world have fully supported all sorts of nationalist movements, large and small, even though Catholicism, by its very name, is supposed to be a universal religion. Communists like Stalin supported the idea of "socialism in a single country" in spite of the fact that communism by its very nature is not supposed to be parochial either. In the final analysis, secular ideologies like democracy, patriotism and communism are not historically founded realities, but just religious doctrines like all the others, whose only useful purpose is to keep people together in various little parochial groupings.

Even the people who support politically correct pressure groups like human rights' organizations and famine relief movements do not really believe in what they are preaching. What are important for the members of these groups are the feel-good ideology which they are supporting and the brownie points that they are accumulating by belonging to such groups. Some professional historians have also written the real histories of some of these groups, showing in an abundance of different cases how prejudiced such groups are: certain human rights and certain famines get much more attention from these organizations than other ones do and always for ideological reasons.

None of the people involved in any of these heritage constructs is actually supposed to really believe in whatever slogan that they happen to be parroting. All of these people are just like the Ba'ath information minister who kept on claiming that Iraqi forces were beating back the enemy even as American forces were successfully occupying Baghdad.

The Big Lie technique was in fact invented long before Joseph Goebbels was born and will certainly continue to be used for many centuries to come. The fact that it currently seems to be used in the USA more often than in any other country is probably just due to the fact that the USA is currently the world's most powerful country. For the heritage crowd, history always has been and always will be just another slogan.

This is why it is so important for history teachers to put the emphasis on developing critical thinking among their students. Teaching history is not just about transmitting useful information to students about how the world came to be the way that it is now. It is more about doubting whatever is being taught at the present time: every history teacher has had the devastating experience of finding out that some particular piece of information that he or she has passed on, from some presumably reliable source, has turned out to be nothing but a figment of some other historian's imagination. Unfortunately, a lot of what is taught in most history courses is just something which some dominant personality wanted others to believe. Totalitarian societies are not the only ones which are continually reinventing their own histories.

COMPETENT EVALUATION

In my first book, I wrote a short chapter about education, in which I tried to make the point that the teaching of professional competency is not contradictory with, but dependent upon, cultural literacy and an emphasis on process and change. In that chapter, I also mentioned my method of teaching history, which is based on the student's comparison between succeeding periods, in all of the different aspects of human life.

What I left out of that discussion was a detailed presentation of the evaluation process involved. How is it possible to figure out if students have really assimilated historical material? This is not only an important topic for history teachers, but is central to the way in which any form of knowledge is transmitted from one person to another. History, after all, is not just a discipline like any one of a hundred others; it is the real queen of the sciences, much more important than physics or philosophy, at least when those subjects are viewed from a static perspective.

While it is true that almost every discipline likes to think of itself as number one, history makes it to the top of the heap for the very simple reason that it includes all the others. Every topic has its own history, since the past, which is history's subject, includes everything which took place before the present or the future: in other words, everything which has ever been written down, talked about, or recorded in any way. Since the present is evanescent and the future is inaccessible, therefore the past is everything, and all the other disciplines are history!

By the same token, a discussion of evaluation in history teaching means nothing less than the discussion of the transmission of all human knowledge, from one human being to another. By looking at history teaching in such an imperialist way, we are of course obliged to reject any attempt which is obviously parochial, or ideologically limited. Any history professor, who is too much under the influence of any particular religion, or any particular country, or any particular point of view, is automatically excluded. If he or she deliberately downplays any aspect of the past, or plays up any particular interpretation of events, then he or she cannot participate in historical hegemony! Once again, such a goal can never be fully achieved, but this should not prevent people from at least trying.

The method I am proposing is the one that I have been using and developing over the past twenty years, in real classrooms. What should a history teacher do when confronted with the need to give a course on some civilization, or country, or period of history, which has been assigned to him or her by whoever does the assigning? The best way to start is to divide all of the essential characteristics of any society into the four categories usually suggested: political history, economic history, social history and cultural history.

Then divide each aspect into two, three or four subordinate categories, in such a way as to attempt to include every major division of the human experience. This is impossible in any absolute sense, but should still be undertaken in order to come as close as possible to a relatively useful result. The end result is about a dozen different categories, that number being chosen for the simple reason that this seems to be the highest number of categories which young adults are capable of handling during any particular fifteen or thirty-week course.

I start by dividing political history into constitutional history (executive, legislative and judicial branches), geopolitical history (wars, treaties, territorial rivalry) and the history of ideologies (the political influence of religion, secular ideologies and political parties or factions). This is a somewhat arbitrary division of political affairs, as are all the other divisions that I have developed, but I believe that they come as close to being all-inclusive as any other group of three political categories.

My division of constitutional history into the three sectors of Montesquieu's eighteenth-century theory of politics is also anachronistic for prior centuries, but the teacher should point out to students what the approximate equivalents are in the ancient world, the Middle Ages, and the early-modern period. Unfortunately, the Euro-centric bias which is part of the same division cannot be helped either, without making the entire method unwieldy and impractical. This should also be pointed out to the students at the beginning of every semester.

In economic history, my task was easier since I simply adopted the classic division between the primary sector (agriculture, pasture, mines, forests and hydrocarbons), the secondary sector (artisan economy, pre-industrial manufacturing and modern industry) and the tertiary sector (commerce, private and public services). This is not an entirely satisfactory division either, but once again it seems to be better than any of the available alternatives.

In social history, I chose social classes (aristocracy, slaves, artisans, serfs, capitalists, workers, middle classes, farmers and so on), women ("ordinary" women as well as "exceptional" women) and minorities (ethnic minorities as well as religious minorities). This division is even more problematical than some of the others, among other reasons because it seems to ignore basic demographic issues such as population changes and the evolution of the family, but I have tried to overcome these weaknesses by talking about population changes within the section on the social classes and about family matters in the section on women. As for those who would deny the very existence of social classes, as Marie Antoinette was supposed to have said, let them eat cake!

Finally, in cultural history, I created one category for all of the arts (literature, music and everything else), another for thought (including philosophy, religious doctrine and the sciences, both natural sciences and social sciences), and a final category for popular culture (folklore, religious ceremonies, spectator sports, mass media, etc.) The first two categories are for the culture of the elite, with the last one reserved for the culture of common folk, which is often, but not always, a useful distinction to make.

Like any general categorization, this one has a number of weaknesses, some of which were mentioned earlier, but I think that these are fewer than with any other possible choice of twelve divisions. Note that religion crops up in several different places, within political ideologies, minorities and cultural affairs, but it is by no means the only element in human history which cuts across these very artificial boundaries.

I then give my courses according to this method. I divide each sub-period of history into twelve sections and I then supply all of the most important or most pertinent information for each category, completing all twelve of them before moving on to the next division of historical time. For example, when teaching the history of Western civilization, I start with the constitutional history of the Ancient World, then the geopolitical history and the history of "ideologies" within that period, before completing the other nine categories. Once the Ancient World has been completed, it is time to move onto the Middle Ages and to cover them in the same way, before taking on the early-modern period (the fifteenth to the eighteenth centuries) and the late-modern, or contemporary period, from the Atlantic Revolutions (1775-1799) to the present.

In this latter endeavor, I do not pretend that it is really possible to teach a competent course on all of Western civilization, from the first Sumerian city-states to the present, from Plato to NATO as the saying goes, in any fifteen-week period. This is, however, the extremely dubious task which the Quebec government has assigned to college teachers (for seventeen and eighteen-year old students), so I try to do the best that I can. I also divide every other history course assigned to me in approximately the same fashion.

In this way, so far as most courses are concerned, a teacher can cover all of the most important information for every period of history, without leaving out anything truly essential. The danger, however, is to leave the students with the impression that each of these different categories is really separate from all the others, or that each of the succeeding periods is really separate from those which precede them, or follow them. All along the way, I have to be constantly pointing out just how arbitrary all these divisions really are and in how many different ways political, economic, social and cultural activities, and succeeding historical periods, are so highly interdependent. There is no way to get around having to analyze the material, by breaking it down into its constituent parts, but the synthetic re-stitching of all the elements back into a complete quilt has to be accomplished before the job is really done. For at least some students, some kind of credible results are at least theoretically possible.

The best way to achieve a unified result is to use a competent method of evaluation. Since history is based on evolution and change, a good form of testing is to require the students to compare succeeding periods of history. Throughout the semester, whether it lasts for only a few weeks or for several months, students should be required to write comparisons, either in short tables or in essay form. In every one of the twelve categories, students should themselves discover which elements within any given category they feel have not changed all that much from one period to the next and which categories they feel have changed drastically. The results should be grouped under separate headings or subtitles, whether the table form or the essay form is used.

To make sure that the links between the categories are also understood, other tests should be devised which put the emphasis on the interdependency of the various aspects of history. In both kinds of tests, the point is to require the students to re-examine their class notes and other accompanying documents so as to themselves discover the dynamics of human life in the real world, to find out that things have not always been the way that they are now and that different choices would have resulted in a far different world. This is why the best kind of tests about the interdependency of categories is based on historiography: get the students to develop their own arguments, based on the data provided, as to why one interpretation of events could be considered better, or worse, than any of the others.

When the teacher corrects all this material, whether comparisons between periods or comparisons between competing points of view, he or she is faced with a daunting assignment. Different students will have come up with different replies, which cannot all just be separated into good answers and bad answers. Two students in the same group, whose answers were significantly different, could still end up getting the same mark. Historians well know how difficult it is to choose between competing interpretations, or between major and minor changes when interpreting historical evolution. Very often, for professional historians as well as for students, a good job will be separated from a poor job not so much by the right or the wrong answer, but by the care which a person has taken to justify his or her choices. None of the sciences nowadays are exact sciences, but history may be the least exact science of them all.

This, by the way, does not make history inferior to any other science, but superior, since false pretensions about exactness are less scientific than fuzzy definitions.

This method that I have chosen is not good just for teaching history. In fact, since every field of knowledge is historically founded, my method can be modified for use in almost every subject. The idea is never to put the emphasis on static series of facts, but instead to stress change or dynamic evolution, the coming into being of knowledge over time, the comparison between a field of inquiry as it is presently set up and what it looked like in days gone by.

This is what the so-called competency-based, or outcomes-oriented, approach should really be all about. It should not just be used so as to provide students with only the minimum, technical education that they need in order to be immediately useful for some private company or another. As I pointed out already in my first book, any competent professional also requires a common cultural background in order to function appropriately in rapidly changing circumstances. The neo-conservative ideology makes a fundamental error when it assumes that people have the right to be ignorant in order to be free, like the "Know-Nothing" Party of the nineteenth-century USA briefly claimed.

It is true, however, that any course, no matter how well planned and executed, turns out to be almost useless if it is taught under ordinary conditions. Even in countries which have adopted the competency method, supposedly based on outcomes, as well as on problem-solving as a replacement for rote learning, schools almost never insist on the material's final assimilation. In many places, the final test has been increased in importance and made to count for 35 or 40% of the final mark. But teachers and professors are not given any additional time at the end of a semester to make a careful final evaluation and the students are still allowed to leave school at the end of the semester without ever having read their final, corrected papers. As a result, the students do not always become aware of any errors that they may have made on the final exercise and will most likely repeat the same mistakes the next time around.

Under these circumstances, education then remains as it always has been which is to say a Sisyphus type of process, in which most of the progress made during any one semester has to be repeated over and over again before it does any good. Even during the same teaching period, one instructor's efforts will be undermined by another teacher's slovenliness, much in the same way that children are disadvantaged if one parent spends all of his or her time working against the influence of the other parent. Students find themselves starting over every semester and every school year, endlessly repeating the same errors.

In fact, if the method that I have outlined in this chapter is to be of any use to the majority of students, schools are going to have to change in the same way that I have recommended that the teaching of history should change. Putting the emphasis on process and evolution is what is should all be about, rather than working ourselves into a Hegelian bad infinity, in which the same stupid thing is allowed to go on forever. If reality can be shown to have a particular history, rather than just describing the coming into being of some predetermined event, then teaching should reflect that fact.

CLASS DENIAL

Another social reality which most North Americans pretend to ignore is the existence of social classes. In decades past, this was pretty hard to do, when major battles were constantly breaking out between organized labor and enormous industrial companies, often involving large police forces, the militia and even the army. In more recent years, however, blue-collar employment in the primary and secondary sectors has been largely replaced by service, or tertiary work, which accounts for about 70% of all the jobs available in any of the Western economies. As a result, organized labor has gone into a continued decline, since it is so much more difficult to organize highly decentralized services. At the same time, a general rise in salaries since the 1950s has made class warfare a somewhat less popular pastime than it used to be, at least in the richer countries.

In the meantime, the communist movement has also largely disappeared from the Western world. As I described it in my first book, the communist parties of days gone by proved to everyone just how irrelevant they were by supporting all sorts of rotten regimes, in which the class struggle between the capitalist bosses and the factory workers was replaced by a class struggle between the communist bosses and the rest of the population. The moral failure of the communist regimes to support the class that they were supposed to be supporting resulted in a world-wide, working-class rejection of the communist option in politics.

Other organizations which used to be close to the factory workers are also declining. All of the socialist and social-democratic parties, which were often elected in various different countries mostly by people who worked for a living, have all turned out to be just as corrupt as the regular, "bourgeois" parties. Labor Party leaders like Harold Wilson and Tony Blair in Great Britain have become leading warmongers as well, and are no longer interested in the working-class at all. Getting elected and staying elected nowadays means keeping as far away from class divisions as possible. Even Brazil's socialist president Lula da Silva does not seem all that interested in the working class any more, at least since he managed to get himself elected.

The irony of all this recent history is that today's world is every bit as divided between social classes as the old one was, and in many ways more so. While the number of service workers is much higher than it used to be, they are still workers and they still do not benefit from economic development nearly as much as their employers do. In fact, the gap between the income levels of the social classes since the Second World War, which was declining in at least a few countries up until the "conservative revolution" of the 1980s, has started to climb again, just like it always had prior to 1945.

The number of industrial workers may also have declined somewhat in places like North America and Western Europe, at least in proportion to the rest of the population, but the rapid industrialization of many parts of the so-called Third World means that the total number of industrial workers on this planet is at an all-time high. Thousands of companies in the richer countries have contributed heavily to this increase in Asian, Latin-American, East-European and even African industrial employment by seeking out low-wage havens in the poorer countries.

Some misguided commentators are also misinterpreting the current decline in collectively organized methods of work, such as Taylorism and the assembly line, in favor of a return to more individual, skill-oriented, methods. They presume that this particular trend in the workplace somehow means that the working-class as a group has ceased to exist, and that everyone has become an ordinary professional nowadays. Back in the nineteenth century, however, before Taylorism was introduced and some skilled workers were making more of their own decisions about how to do industrial work, no one was talking about the decline of the working-class as an identifiable group. The division of society into social classes does not depend on the size of the workplace or on the methods being used, or even on the realization among individuals that they belong to such and such a class. It depends on the relative allocations of power and wealth all over the world.

At the same time, none of the rotten ways in which a few people manage to get rich, and stay rich, have declined either, on the contrary. All of the recent scandals concerning Enron, WorldCom and a couple of thousand other such companies are just the tip of the proverbial iceberg, while millions of people are still suffering from engineered bankruptcies all the time. Almost every company on the planet, from the very largest right down to the smallest, is now, always has been and always will be heavily involved in all sorts of illegal and immoral activities. There is no way to make money on a large scale, either initially or over a long period of time, without committing the world's most disgusting acts of hatred toward other people.

This is why "ethical investment" is such a huge scam, since there is no way to separate the good part of capitalism from the bad part. Even totalitarian countries which deliberately attempt to become self-sufficient never succeed in cutting themselves off completely from all the other countries. Since at least the end of the nineteenth century, the world economy has become so intertwined, in so many different ways, that no one investment can ever be completely separated from any other investment. Investors have as much chance of remaining ethical as nationalists have in encouraging people to buy only local products ("Buy America"). Boycotting other people's capital is as foolish as boycotting other people's products, as American patriots found out when they tried to boycott "Canada Dry" after the recent war on Iraq, only to find out that the soft-drink company does not belong to the Canadian pacifists but to a group of British investors.

The lack of ethics also explains why courts can still get away with disallowing such things as union work-to-rule campaigns, in which those labor organizations which still exist periodically try to put pressure on their bosses by trying to cut down on compulsory overtime, unsafe working conditions, poor treatment of customers and suppliers, and so on. A work-to-rule campaign depends on the fact that the employer, or the government, has already recognized the illegality or the unfairness of each one of these horrible on-the-job practices. But when unions try to enforce what are presumably already-accepted rules of behavior, the courts always

135

grant injunctions in order to force the workers to do whatever the employers want them to do, over and above the so-called rules. This is just another example of ordinary people having their rights until they need them, since in reality all human rights ultimately belong to the employers and not to anyone else.

The Titanic tragedy of 1912, in which it seems that most of the working-class people were deliberately drowned while most of the bourgeois people were saved, has become a microcosm of capitalist society. Thousands of similar incidents are still taking place all the time, like the chemical explosion in Bhopal, India, in 1984. The most recent movie about the Titanic did a good job, at least part of the time, in depicting as accurately as possible what happens to people during events of that kind.

What was important to most of the people involved in these disasters, even to many of those in the greatest danger of dying, was not the fact that the disaster was taking place and that as many people should be saved as possible. Instead, decorum had to be preserved at all costs, in other words the overwhelming urge to maintain class divisions, domination and hierarchy, no matter what was happening in the material world. Physical reality was not really important, nor was biological existence; only social patterns had any real significance. As for those who resisted that kind of evil, as the nineteenth-century American industrialist, Henry Frick, used to say: "I can always get one half of the working-class to beat up the other half".

This kind of attitude still dominates most people's thinking even today. As a result slavery is also on the rise. Even though that particular institution has been illegal everywhere on the globe since Mauritania became the last country to ban it back in 1980, this has not prevented several hundred million people, mostly women and children, from living in slavery. Many of these people work every day in agriculture, industry and ordinary services, while countless others are forced into prostitution. Millions of workers are still being killed all the time in various, highly-preventable workplace accidents, while millions of others are still being run over and shot down during violent strikes and social rebellions. On a world scale, none of the rotten social conditions that the socialist and the communist parties of old used to denounce all the time have declined, quite the contrary.

In Marxist jargon, this means that the objective conditions for a world socialist revolution have never been riper, while the subjective conditions have never been more dismal. In other words, the working classes in most countries are more exploited and mistreated than they ever were, but the social and political organizations which were supposed to change all that have never been weaker or more discredited. In spite of all this decline, however, the many unions and worker-oriented political parties that still exist go on being as corrupt as ever, protecting criminals and other toxic personalities in their midst as much as protecting the people who need their services. As with so many other human problems, this one does not seem to have any readily available solutions.

Class division is after all based on social competition, rather than on cooperation. Even though every sort of material and moral benefit in the world comes from cooperation, without which no human institutions could function, competition has still become the prevailing moral "value" in society. Pollyannas may say that it does not matter whether someone wins or loses, but it does matter how that person plays the game. In reality, however, a successful competitor in the world oligopoly gets to make important decisions about everyone's future, while an unsuccessful competitor loses control over everything. This is certainly very depressing for the loser, while the winner is in what is at least morally an even worse situation, since he or she belongs to the group of people causing most of the world's troubles. Luckily for us all (!), most winners do not have any moral scruples, so society goes stumbling nicely along.

Some foolish people, such as anarchists, nihilists and hippies left over from the Peace and Love generation, still think that "bourgeois" rules are the root of all evil, and that if only everyone was free to do whatever he or she pleased, the world would be a great place for everyone. In fact, however, real bourgeois people, in other words major investors, never obey any of the bourgeois "rules" which get the hippies so upset. Their only long-term rule is to do whatever is necessary for them to come out on top.

As a result, the dominating class of people ends up consuming a hugely disproportionate share of the world's goods and services, while managing to avoid most of the work. The dominated classes, of course, have to compensate by doing exactly the opposite. Once launched into society by the ruling classes, this spoiled-brat syndrome then becomes the psychological basis on which millions of other freeloaders get away with avoiding all of their responsibilities.

In today's world, in spite of living in a society which is more individualistic than it was before, people still have to live on the same planet with all the other people. Self-definition may be a source of freedom in theory, but the anxiety produced by cutting oneself off from everyone else (Durkheim's anomie) is more a source of suicidal tendencies than anything else. People still cluster together in groups nowadays as much as they ever did.

Unfortunately, whenever humans get together on some project or another, they invariably create social hierarchy and eventually social classes where none seemed to exist before. Even a department of ten or twenty professors hired for the first time at some newly-founded university will inevitably separate into groups of dominant individuals and groups of dominated individuals after only several weeks of normal operations. Toxic personalities will inevitably emerge, taking over prestigious tasks such as research and publication, and leaving the teaching of freshman classes to those possessing some sort of social conscience.

Once the initial division has been set into place, the dominant individuals will use the worker-bees over-work as a method of staying on top by denying others the time necessary to develop any of the more prestigious skills. Before long, instead of actually doing any research or publishing anything interesting, the toxic personalities will simply get together in committees designed to make it seem that they are working harder than everyone else. These committees will then come up with a series of recommendations as to how to preserve the initial division of labor by getting the overworked under-class to work even harder. Most of the time, no one at all will end up doing any useful research or publishing anything of any importance, while the students will inevitably be shoved together into oversized classes. In this example as in all the others, the division of labor inevitably becomes more important to the people involved than the labor itself.

However, pointing out that social classes do indeed exist, and are constantly being created and recreated anew, should not be construed as support for some kind of left-wing or pro-socialist point of view. The fact is that most socialist and communist politicians have been just as disgusting in their behavior towards the "inferior" classes in society as liberal and conservative politicians have. For example, when Douglas Casey described foreign aid as a transfer from poor people in rich countries to rich people in poor countries, he was simply describing another way in which left-liberal politicians mistreat poor people as much as populist conservatives do.

So the illusion that twenty-first century society is rapidly becoming more and more egalitarian, or more and more democratic, is not borne out by any observations in the real world. People in the richer countries are always forgetting that class analysis has to be world-wide in scope in order to be realistic. Even when it is real, partial social reconciliation in some countries is more than offset by increasing division in other countries. Real democracy is in fact no more possible than real communism, or real racial equality, or real gender equality. Many people's outlooks on this matter may be a lot cloudier and more confused than they used to be, but social division itself, while less obvious in some places, is as real today as it ever was.

WHAT VACATION?

The institution known as the vacation has to be one of the most absurd aspects of modern society. This is the annual, or semi-annual, ritual by which most middle-class people in the richer countries spend somewhere between one and five weeks a year on some kind of prolonged leisure activity at a designated summer or winter vacation spot. True, the majority of people on this planet are still too poor to even think of such a thing, since they spend their entire lives either picking someone else's garbage or working non-stop for the benefit of some well-to-do slave-owner. A few other people (the slave-owners) do not really work at all and are therefore unable to stop jet-setting long enough to appreciate what going on vacation might feel like by contrast with working. But there are still hundreds of millions of people in between these two extremes who have made vacationing into what it has now become.

Unfortunately, almost all of the designated vacation spots are now so overcrowded that vacation time has become a dubious proposition at best. Putting a large number of people onto the public highways or airports at the same time, to go to the same beaches, or the same cathedrals, or the same ski slopes, on the same weeks of the year, is a recipe for disaster. People end up spending most of their designated relaxation time eating each other's gasoline fumes, waiting in line or following each other about from one partly visible painting or sculpture to another.

No one writing tourist guidebooks ever explains to the readers how they are supposed to be appreciating great contributions to civilization when only about half of any given object can ever be seen by anyone in the crowd. How are all of the tourists supposed to concentrate on the

140

meaning of an object, or on its historical context, when hundreds of other people close at hand are listening to dozens of human and mechanical guides describing the same objects at a dozen different rhythms and in a dozen different languages?

Meanwhile, down at the beach, some unfortunate tourists may even end up coming face to feces with some other tourist's excrement while they are supposed to be playing in the water. Although many of the more modern beaches are often cleaned every morning, this does not prevent bathers and boaters from sharing each other's waste matter in the afternoon, particularly in such Earthly paradises as southern California and the French Riviera.

In the meantime, all of the world-class cultural monuments and natural sites are slowly being eroded away bit by bit, by all of the Neanderthals and Cro-Magnons who come to visit them so often. Like the tomb raiders on American television, most of these people think nothing of taking home a few chunks of world-class material for show-and-tell with their friends and neighbors. By the time the hundreds of millions of Third World wage-slaves become rich enough to go on vacation themselves, there may not be any world-class sites left to visit. Not to mention those unfortunate sites in war-torn areas all over the world, in which the looting of cultural booty has always been a very lucrative pastime.

Nevertheless, today's ordinary visitors are being politely asked to help preserve the environment while simultaneously getting packed like sardines into tight little containers (airplanes and automobiles, among other pleasure craft), dumped into cute little goulags for collective restoration and accommodation, and then shunted into tight little lines leading up to the monuments or down to the beaches. Such people are also being asked to pay a very large percentage of their annual incomes for the pleasure of treading on each other's toes and listening to each other's radio commercials.

In many cases, vacation has turned out to the most stressful period of a person's year, since he or she is expected to pay out good money in order to do things that normally he or she would expect to receive good money in order to tolerate. The vacation world ends up being the exact opposite of the workday world, with the number of pleasurable experiences often being higher at work than on time-off.

CIVILIZED SEX

Sex is another leisure-time activity which often suffers from the syndrome of great expectations, a large number of people expecting to get more out of it than they put into it! As with the vacation, however, not yet everybody is allowed to participate. In many old-fashioned societies, which are often replicated inside the ghettos of all major cities, sexual activity is still under severe social control and does not usually get beyond procreation. A large number of people, however, have managed to move on out of their traditional, cultural cages and are now able to join in the fun, so to speak.

Civilized sex begins when modern society allows it to begin, but the results are still often incomplete (the pun is intended). For one thing, civilized sex is much more of a two-way street than it used to be, with women being allowed to participate much more than they did in the past. By itself, this is a major step forward, provided that the people involved have adjusted their old-fashioned Neolithic attitudes to modern life.

The biggest problem still remaining is machismo, namely the idea that men are inevitably tough, dominant creatures whose needs can and should be quickly satisfied. This erroneous view has led to all sorts of rotten experiences, even among people who have gotten beyond the feudal fixation on covering up women's faces and bodies completely, on the ridiculous assumption that all men are always and forever in heat. In fact, only pathetic machos really behave in this way, and only equally pathetic bimboes can really get down to the same lower depths. Unfortunately, machismo also applies as much to homosexual sex as it does to the heterosexual kind, particularly in the case of those disgusting

142

individuals who insist on sharing their sexually-transmitted diseases with as many other people as possible.

But the belief that all real men are perpetual sex-heads is still to be found even among some modern, enlightened women who enjoy and expect full participation and satisfaction. Even psychologically mature and egalitarian women sometimes find themselves being attracted to macho musclemen with tiny brains and inadequate performances. For these unfortunate women, the superficial sex-appeal of a hard-body, shown off in public, is more important than any of the sensitivity, the charm or even the bedroom capacities of the men that they pretend to prefer.

These women are still capable of periodically downgrading their own standards in order to make it with some caveman, preferably in the most disgusting circumstances possible. Unfortunately, many of these people, from both sexes, are only capable of being fully aroused by getting down in the dirt and playing with the pigs. Apparently, the worse the situation gets, the greater the high that results.

Another fascinating contradiction among some other middle-class women is their expectation that even in the richer countries and regions of the world, even where sexual activity has become entirely consensual and non-sexist men are still expected to be chivalrous. Unfortunately for that idea, chivalry was invented so that young knights in the Middle Ages would not mistreat those aristocratic women whose husbands had gone off to the Crusades. It has no place whatsoever in modern, middle-class life, especially in those blessed countries and professions, in which men and women do the same jobs, get paid the same salaries and share the housework equally. (This last form of equality is still rare, however.) Chivalry is also particularly inappropriate since women are now living ten to fifteen years longer than men, rather than the other way around which used to be true back when chivalry was invented.

Oddly enough, some people also project the differences between the sexes onto social and political behavior. They assume that such exceptionally powerful women as Margaret Thatcher are somehow too masculine, since they have been seen starting wars and breaking strikes. But all of those women, who have been given half a chance to prove themselves, whether recently or in past centuries, have always ended up being as disgustingly "masculine" as any of the male rulers who mistreat other people all the time.

In reality, women are just as capable as men at being toxic personalities, as all those "powerless" women prove whenever they so enthusiastically encourage their men-folk to go off and get themselves killed during wartime.

None of this, however, can justify the way that most women on this planet are still being treated by their men. All over the world, but particularly in the poorest parts of it, thousands of women are still being killed every year, for extremely minor offenses, ostensibly in order to uphold some tribal society's "honor". It is fascinating to reflect on the psychology of such people, those who still believe that murder is an honorable act. Millions of other women are also being punished for their own attractiveness, among other things by having acid thrown in their faces. Their "crimes" are as minor as being seen in public without being accompanied by a chaperone and have nothing whatever to do with the gluttonous behavior being encouraged among the jet-set.

The least that can be said is that civilized sex, and civilized attitudes toward the differences between the sexes, are still a long way off and do not seem to be getting any closer. This is really unfortunate, since nothing can be more fun than participating in sexual activity with a partner who is entirely present and accounted for. The same sort of positive appreciation also applies to any other shared activity between men and women.

RHETORICAL QUESTION MARKS

A rhetorical question is supposed to be a question whose answer is obvious, understood and contained within the question itself. What often happens, however, is that the rhetoric, which is to say the method of expression, often becomes more important than the message being delivered. Marshall Macluhan, in fact, did not discover much when he came up with the idea that the medium is the message, since that sort of idea has always been implicit in the rhetorical method taught in most European universities over the centuries.

This sort of thing often becomes clear whenever people write Master's or Ph. D. theses. A student embarking on such a project may initially believe his or her thesis director's opening remarks, to the effect that when carrying out a scientific inquiry, it does not matter at all whether or not the results uphold the student's initial hypothesis, force him or her to reject that hypothesis, or in some cases are not sufficiently conclusive to support either a positive or a negative decision concerning that hypothesis. Theoretically, this is indeed the kind of instruction which should be given, since a scientific inquiry is supposed to be open-ended so far as results are concerned. Unfortunately, the subsequent behavior of the thesis director or the jury which grants the degree does not often conform to those instructions.

In fact, as many students find out to their horror, a positive result is much more pleasing to the director of the thesis, to the department and to the university involved, than is a negative or an inconclusive result. If the student insists on carrying out his or her research in as scientific a way as possible, his or her career may be compromised. Quite often, in order to prevent such an event from taking place, the department may "suggest" to the candidate that he or she should adopt a more rhetorical approach to the subject.

When this happens, rhetoric turns out to be a substitute for insufficient evidence. Rather than admitting that no conclusion can be made, or that the initial hypothesis should simply be rejected, the student may be called upon to fiddle with his or her hypothesis so that the "subsequent" results are upheld, with a more positive outcome. In that case, the department and the university can be seen as having supposedly contributed more to the ongoing progress of science than other departments or other universities have.

Theoretically, all possible results contribute to science equally, at least if the researcher has not made any important errors. In the case of a negative result, researchers in a particular field know that is it futile to attempt to prove that particular hypothesis, so another one has to be discovered. In the case of an inconclusive result, researchers are informed that the available evidence cannot be dealt with using that type of hypothesis. Both of these results are supposed to be just as scientific as a positive result, but in the real world of university and departmental competition, a proven hypothesis looks so much better.

The temptation is therefore to short-circuit the entire process by getting a student to change his or her initial hypothesis as soon as possible, which is to say as soon as it becomes obvious that the researcher is not finding sufficient evidence to prove the original educated guess. Those other students who hear about such goings-on are often tempted to avoid all such problems by choosing safe subjects, in which the evidence is already abundant. When this happens, people end up "proving" propositions which seem entirely superfluous. Prizes for excellence, and the academic positions that often accompany them, are then awarded to those students whose only real glory is to have underlined something that everyone knew was obvious from the beginning.

The medium then becomes the message, at least for the student. And the message which is being sent out is simple: the content of the scientific process is not what is important. What is important is the competition between professors in a department for the most "successful" students, the competition between departments for the most successful theses and the competition between universities for the greatest "advances" in science.

This rhetorical progress is also intensified when a thesis director criticizes a student's text for its lack of conviction. This is where the old Jesuit definition of rhetoric comes into play. According to this theory, whenever a student is writing a thesis, the professor or team of professors assigned to help the student are not only there to ensure that the thesis obeys all the proper rules for scientific investigation.

At some point, the rhetoric involved becomes more important than the process of discovery. The thesis director's job is transformed into confronting the student with feigned, or phony, opposition. Even if the department entirely agrees with the object of the thesis, the professors assigned to that student are supposed to find artificial fault with each of the different chapters, over and above the real problems that they uncover. The object is to create a debate between the student and the thesis director (or directors) so that the student will be obliged to defend his or her work and its accompanying hypothesis against all comers. The idea seems to be that the jury, which is composed mainly of colleagues other than the thesis director, often from other universities, will be inclined to be harsh with the candidate, in the interests of science, and that the director therefore has to prepare his or her candidate for this future event by feigning opposition in advance.

If the student falters, if he or she has any lingering doubts about the fecundity of the hypothesis, or about the adequacies of the research, then these will presumably be revealed during the rhetorical debate. Unfortunately, this whole process reinforces everyone's desire to come up with a positive result and often skews the whole scientific inquiry completely.

This kind of rhetorical process favors those students who like taking shortcuts, either by choosing an easy subject or by coming up with a hypothesis which is so devoid of content that almost any "evidence" would uphold it. On the other hand, the honest student who has chosen a difficult subject to analyze and who does not feel that the evidence collected justifies a positive interpretation of the hypothesis, will then often wilt under the feigned cross-examination and admit to his or her thesis director that the results of the research are not going to be positive.

When that happens, the director and the jury will usually be biased against that particular candidate. They may decide to refuse to admit the thesis, in extreme cases, or to admit it only with certain reservations. They may also decide to accept the thesis, but then give the student a mark which is lower than an "A". Unfortunately, if any of those decisions are taken, the student can kiss his or her future career good-bye, since in almost every field, there are more than enough unreserved "A" students to cover all the available university postings.

For the scientific discipline involved, this results in a large number of practically useless theses which do not really prove anything heretofore unknown and a small number of difficult and maligned theses which lack the elegance of a positive proof. Fields of inquiry in which hypotheses are often difficult to prove, such as the social sciences, may end up being worse off at the end of the process than they were at the beginning. At the same time, many academics who become a discipline's leading "researchers" are very often overrated.

Abominations like this can easily take place even in a university setting, where scientific inquiry is supposed to be everyone's main goal. But rhetorical substitutes for content crop up even more often in non-scientific institutions. The courtroom is a rather obvious example. Millions of cases have been won over the years by lawyers who are skilled in convincing others of the validity of their interpretations without the benefit of a great deal of evidence. Most judges, who were once lawyers themselves, are a lot like most professors, in that they enjoy an elegant argument more than they enjoy a difficult decision. Judges and juries are constantly being swayed in every which direction by lawyers whose main claim to fame is their capacity to convince rather than their capacity to uncover legal precedents. The results are even worse than those of the academic world: rhetoric triumphs even more often over reality. What an accused person, or company, actually did, or did not do, ends up being much less important than the rhetorical "case" which his lawyer has brought before the court.

Another fascinating example of this same problem is in the work of psychoanalysis. Following Freud's prescriptions, most psychoanalysts are not so much interested in helping the patient as in finding out how their patients came to have the psychological difficulties that they are experiencing. But this often leads the so-called therapist into becoming much more interested in just how the patient fits into the various categories of psychological disorders that the analysts have discovered or invented over the years. Instead of simply getting the patient to stay away from the toxic personalities who often caused their problem initially, psychoanalysts usually try to get their patients to admit their own guilty mistakes and to work their problems out for themselves. In this case, the therapist ends up identifying with the perpetrator, against the victim, just like in the courtroom.

Business is probably the world's best, or worst, example of this sort of thing, for the simple reason that there are very few institutional barriers for disinformation. Universities, courts and psychoanalysts are at least glumly supposed to be truthful, while business leaders are instead enthusiastically encouraged to profit from other people's weaknesses. How many products become successful on the market not because of their intrinsic worth, but because of the quality of the marketing schemes? The classic example from the 1980s was the commercial war between IBM and Apple computers, in which the inferior product won the hearts of consumers much more than it won their minds. The same comparison also applies to most current software.

Insider trading is also not so much the exception to the rule as the rule itself. How is anyone in business supposed to make any money if that person is not allowed to profit from some information for which other people do not have equal access? Making rules against insider trading is hypocritical, since that is what all possible money-making schemes are based upon. Punishing inside traders is just fining the more obvious perpetrators for something which all business people must inevitably do.

Rhetoric in a university, courtroom or psychoanalytical setting is also analogous to the avoidance of competition in business. Investors avoid reality not only by manipulating consumers, but also by banding together to avoid lowering their prices. Although in economics textbooks, businesses are supposed to benefit the consumer by competing among themselves for sales, in reality most firms succeed in avoiding competition by using all sorts of different methods. The recent shenanigans of the Enron, WorldCom, etc., etc., business executives are simply the latest examples of the creative ways in which more outrageous lying replaces the less outrageous kind.

News broadcasts which are nothing but disguised entertainment shows are still another good example. In this case, entertainment is considered to be at least as important as hard news, precisely because the latter is too hard and most people no longer want to put up with reality. In fact, news broadcasts have always been much more propaganda than reality, but at least people in days gone by were not always arguing that burlesque was as important as war or poverty.

Unfortunately, the victory of marketing over substance has become so important nowadays that many people are claiming that the difference between rhetoric and reality is a bogus difference. For them, marketing, categorization, legal pleading and elegant theses are at least as important to society as are utility, therapy, degree of guilt and fundamental discovery. These are the people for whom every "competence" is as important as every other one, every kind of person is necessary to make up a world and every component of a system is as much a part of the whole as any other component.

Without realizing it, these people "reason" in the same way that incompetent students unsuccessfully attempt to analyze course material. Many students are completely unable to answer exam questions properly because they cannot distinguish between the main theme of a text and its secondary content. For them, every little piece of information is as important as every other little piece. For example, they think that the Great Depression of the 1930s was caused just as much by the stock market crash of 1929 as it was by the growing gap between the ever-expanding productive capacity of the economy and the stagnant purchasing power of the majority of the population. For them, as for certain economists, big things and little things are just things.

In the real world, however, fundamental causes are more important than immediate causes, product quality is more important than marketing, therapy is more important than categorization, the degree of guilt is more important than rhetorical flourishes, and the scientific method is more important than verbal elegance. Those who insist on believing in the opposite are for the most part professional liars, whose very existence depends on the dominance of flimflam. Unfortunately for them, human society can only put up with so much unreality before it starts to come apart at the seams. World wars, economic depressions and ecological catastrophes have been the usual result in the past and new catastrophes are still pending nowadays.

The difference between major themes and minor themes is like the difference between magic and science, or the difference between curing infectious diseases by the casting of spells or by using penicillin. Ultimately, it is the difference between really curing the patient and letting the patient get a whole lot worse. In every one of these different areas—academic research, law, psychotherapy, business and economics—a given society can put up with a great deal of garbage before it finally breaks down. But no one really knows how much is too much.

For these reasons, taking the lying out of living ought to become the most important crusade of them all. Unfortunately for me, however, my method of universal skepticism prevents me from ending this book on such a high note!